GAME COOKERY

GAME
COOKERY

by E. N. and Edith Sturdivant

Outdoor Life · New York

Library of Congress Catalog Card Number 67-13724

Manufactured in the United States of America

CONTENTS

Introduction

In this book on the cooking of game, we intend to stress simple ways of preparing it in an appetizing manner. This is not a cookbook for gourmets. We do not soak the game for hours in a soda or brine solution, nor do we marinate it in wines or fancy sauces, or add numerous exotic herbs. We treat the game as you would a choice piece of beef and stress simple every-day home cooking methods. We have cooked and eaten tons of game meat, and on rare occasions we have used wine. We also use certain herb seasonings, but only to bring out to the fullest extent the distinctive flavor of each species of game. Each recipe is the result of numerous experiments, taking away a little of this, adding a little of that, until we arrived at a satisfactory result. We are confident that by following the basic principles in each recipe, the result will be a savory dish accepted and enjoyed by the entire family.

Throughout the book the pronoun *we* refers to my wife, who perfected these recipes. I was her guinea pig, and as a consequence I am somewhat overweight!

When we invite friends to dinner, we nearly always serve game of some kind. Knowing their compliments to have been sincere, it was at the insistence of many friends that we began to prepare this book. We also feel that there is a real place for such a cookbook. How many times we have heard the remark, "Oh, we have our freezer full of game—but I don't know how to cook it so the family will eat it." There are probably tons of delicious game meat in freezers today, of which the great part will find its way to the garbage can simply because of a notion that there is some deep, dark secret about making it into a tasty dish.

It is surprising how many people stare at us in disbelief when we tell them that approximately ninety percent of the meat we consume is game. With so many tasty ways of preparation we never seem to tire of it, and after a few days on beef we really look forward to returning to our usual diet.

1

·At the local market one may choose among beef, pork, lamb, fowl, fish and an assortment of cold meats. In our own freezer you would find deer, elk, antelope and quite often moose, along with grouse, pheasant, quail and other game birds. Or how would you like a nice grain-fed mallard or a blue-winged teal for dinner? Maybe you would prefer a mess of white-winged or mourning doves. You prefer fish? We can offer fresh-water bass or catfish fried Southern style with hushpuppies. Or maybe you would rather have a nice Montana trout à la Sturdivant! For a change there will be frog legs or turtle. You've never eaten turtle? Then you don't know what you're missing!

An infinite number of dishes can be prepared with venison. Would you like a touch of Italy in your dinner tonight? Then we suggest venison meat balls and spaghetti. If you want to go to a little more trouble, try stuffed rigatoni, served with a good red wine. It is delicious! Should you want to make a culinary journey south of the border, we suggest tamales, chili con carne, or a tamale pie; or you can delight the entire family by serving merry-go-round tacos. For all of these dishes venison is unsurpassed.

A New England boiled dinner using corned venison is so superior to corned beef that there is no comparison, and the corning process is simple and easy. You will find venison mincemeat superb. We have all of this, plus jerked venison smoked with mesquite wood, also "jerky" that has been sun-dried Indian style. We can also offer you at least four different kinds of smoked venison sausage. With so many different ways of preparing venison, you can hardly tire of it.

There is always some kind of game in season, and if the man of the house is an outdoorsman he should be able to provide the family with game the year round.

We have tried to keep the recipes both simple and appealing. Don't be afraid to experiment a little. Perhaps you will wish to leave out some seasoning we have suggested, or to add one that you are especially fond of.

You will probably notice a touch of the South in some of the recipes, especially in the accompanying dishes we recommend. Well, I was born and reared in the South, and as I have said, this is a cookbook not for gourmets but for those who like good home-style cooking. But there is one thing we cannot overstress: that no matter how good a cook you are, unless the game is properly cared for after the kill, all your culinary skill will be in vain. So we suggest to the hunter of the household that he carefully read the section on What to Do After the Kill. If he does that, the rest is easy.

Part I

GAME ANIMALS

Whitetail Deer

Of the several species of deer living in North America, the commonest, the Virginia white-tailed deer, is the most widely hunted big game animal in America. It is found all the way from coast to coast, and from Canada south to Peru. On the average, it isn't as large as the Western mule deer, although bucks weighing more than 275 pounds are sometimes killed, usually near the Canadian border.

The first specimen to be scientifically described was taken in 1784 in Virginia, whence the common name of Virginia white-tailed deer. When one is startled the most prominent part to be seen as it runs through the woods and brush is the feathery snow-white tail standing straight up. In winter its coat takes on a bluish-gray color like that of the mule deer.

The white-tailed deer was a valuable asset to the pioneers of America, providing both food and skins, which were used for clothing and other purposes. During the mid-seventeen hundreds, over half a million deerskins were shipped to England from Georgia. Had it not been such a prolific animal, usually giving birth to twins and occasionally to triplets, within a few years it might have become almost extinct, as did the great herds of buffalo that once roamed the plains.

By the end of the Colonial period, all the colonies except Georgia had enacted legislation protecting the deer, setting an open season and a bag limit. It is interesting to note that as early as 1694 there were men in Massachusetts with enough vision to see the need for such legislation, so that it became the first state to pass laws controlling the slaughter of deer.

Western Mule Deer

The mule deer is found in practically all the Western states, from Washington to Texas and from Montana and Wyoming to southern California, as well as in the seemingly barren deserts of Arizona and old Mexico.

A field dressed specimen weighing 275 pounds is not unusual, and some near the 400-pound mark have been reported.

The heaviest of these deer will be found in Montana, Wyoming and Colorado, but those with the largest antlers—or "racks," as they are called by sportsmen—have been found in the Kaibab National Forest of Arizona.

The best time to hunt mule deer is early in the morning before they bed down, or late in the afternoon, just before sunset, at the start of another major feeding period.

Some hunters of white-tailed deer look down upon the mule deer with disdain as a stupid animal, not nearly as smart as the white-tail. In the past few years, increased hunting pressure has forced mule deer to become much smarter. In a short time you may have reason to think they are just as smart as the elk, or wapiti—and nobody calls them stupid.

VENISON LOIN ROAST

4 pounds venison loin roast   Salt
5 narrow slices beef suet,   Pepper
   one inch thick

Salt and pepper the meat on all sides, rubbing it in well. Place the sliced beef suet on the meat, holding it in place with toothpicks, and place on a rack in a roasting pan. Bake twenty minutes per pound in a preheated oven at 325 degrees. This will give you a juicy, tasty medium-rare roast. If desired, gravy may be made from the drippings in the roasting pan. Blend two tablespoons of flour into a cup of water and pour into the roasting pan, stirring constantly and slowly adding warm water until the desired thickness is reached. Salt and pepper to taste.

Serve with baked potatoes, green peas, French bread or hard rolls, and a Caesar salad. For dessert we suggest lemon pie or jello. This will serve four to six people.

BROILED VENISON CHOPS

Even if you do not own a barbecue stand, you can still give broiled chops the flavor of wood smoke. This recipe is also a good one for weather when you can't cook out on the lawn or patio.

2 venison chops, approximately   1 cup melted butter
  one inch thick, per serving   ¼ cup liquid smoke

Brush liquid smoke on both sides of the chops and let them stand for thirty minutes or longer.

Cover a broiler pan with heavy aluminum foil, brush melted butter on top side of chops and put them under the broiler. Do not place them too close to the flame or the butter will ignite. Cook for about eight minutes; then turn the chops, baste them generously with melted butter, and cook for approximately five minutes more. This should give you a medium rare chop, tender, juicy and with a slight taste of wood smoke. Remove and salt and pepper to taste.

Either baked potatoes, with sour cream and chives, or French fries, plus a tossed green salad, hot French garlic bread, and a good burgundy wine at room temperature are excellent with this meal. Serves six people.

CHARCOAL BROILED VENISON CHOPS

Venison chops cooked over charcoal or under the broiler are far superior to any method of pan-frying.

**12 venison chops, approximately   1 cup melted butter
    one inch thick**

Let charcoal fire burn down to a clean white ash. Brush chops on both sides with melted butter and place on grill. Keep grill high enough from coals to prevent too rapid cooking. Cook about eight minutes, turn and baste again generously with melted butter. About six minutes on this side should suffice, depending upon how well done you like your meat. Keep it on the rare or medium rare side, and you will have a more tender, juicy, and flavorsome piece of meat. When done, remove from fire and salt and pepper to taste.

Serve with baked potatoes with sour cream and chives, or with French fries if you prefer, and a crisp green salad with your favorite dressing. We prefer toast or warm garlic bread with this meal. The recipe serves six.

VENISON LOIN OR BACKSTRAP AU JUS

Quite often, in processing deer, we remove the loin or "backstrap" from the backbone so as to save room in the freezer. This gives a choice piece of boneless meat, the length depending upon the size of the deer. Properly cooked, it is tender, juicy and very flavorsome. This means cooking slowly over a low fire; otherwise it will be dry and tough.

**6 slices loin, approximately   1 tablespoon bacon fat or cook-
    one inch thick   ing oil
    (allow three per person)   Salt
                                 Pepper**

Place the bacon fat or cooking oil in a heavy skillet and heat it over low fire. Salt and pepper both sides of the meat, place in the skillet and cover with a loose-fitting lid; an inverted pie plate will do. Cook approximately five minutes, turn, and cook five minutes on the other side. Remove the meat to a heated platter. While the skillet is hot, pour in one-fourth to one-half cup of water, and simmer with the juices and residue of the meat. Spoon this juice over mashed or baked potatoes.

VENISON BACKSTRAP AND CREAM GRAVY

Here is a hearty breakfast that will stick to your ribs until noon, whether you are at work or in search of some elusive game.

3 pieces venison backstrap per person	Salt
Cooking oil	Pepper
	Flour
	Milk

Salt and pepper the meat and dredge thoroughly in flour. Place in a heavy skillet into which you have poured cooking oil to a depth of approximately a quarter inch. Cover with an inverted pie plate and cook over a medium fire for approximately eight minutes, or until light brown. Remove the pie plate, turn the meat and cook until the other side is brown. Remove the meat to a platter and add two tablespoons of flour to the skillet, stirring constantly until it browns. Add milk and continue to stir until the gravy is of the desired thickness. When it bubbles, add salt and pepper to taste.

Serve with piping hot biscuits.

VENISON LOIN AND EGGS

This is a man's breakfast dish, very similar to the steak and egg breakfast you often find on the menu in Western restaurants.

2 pieces of venison loin per serving	Flour
2 eggs per serving	Salt
	Pepper

Slice the loin approximately half an inch thick. Salt, pepper and sprinkle with flour. Pound in the seasoning by striking lightly with a meat mallet. Place in a well-oiled heavy skillet over a medium fire. Cover with an inverted pie plate and leave to brown five minutes. Remove the pie plate, turn, and cook on the other side for five minutes. Remove meat and drop the eggs into the skillet, add two or three drops of water and cover with the pie plate once again. Steam the eggs three minutes without turning. Place the meat and eggs on a plate garnished with a thin slice of orange.

Serve with hot biscuits, butter and honey.

CHICKEN-FRIED VENISON STEAK

¾ pound venison round steak	Milk
½ cup pancake mix	Salt
2 tablespoons bacon fat or cooking oil	Pepper

Pound the steak on both sides with a meat mallet, and add salt and pepper. Make a medium thick batter, using milk with pancake mix. Dip meat in batter, coating it thoroughly. Heat bacon fat or cooking oil in heavy skillet to a medium heat. Place meat in skillet, cover and cook eight to ten minutes. Remove cover, turn meat and cook approximately five minutes more. Be sure the fire is not too hot. A hot fire and overcooking makes venison dry, tough and tasteless.

Serve with cooked dried beans, a green vegetable, and a salad of sliced tomatoes and onion in oil and vinegar. For dessert we suggest pie or ice cream.

This recipe should serve two hearty eaters.

VENISON SWISS STEAK NO. 1

2 pounds venison round steak cut three-quarters of an inch thick	Salt
	Pepper
	Garlic salt
1 medium-size onion, chopped	Flour
1 small green pepper, chopped	Bacon fat or cooking oil
1 teaspoon Worcestershire sauce	

Salt, pepper and dredge the steak in flour. If you think the venison may be tough, pound it with a meat mallet.

In bacon fat or cooking oil, sear meat well on both sides, until the skillet is well coated with browned flour. If necessary, add more flour to the meat. When flour is well browned, add Worcestershire sauce and sprinkle with garlic salt, salt and pepper. Then add onion and green pepper, with enough water to cover the meat. Simmer until the meat is tender, adding water if necessary to keep the gravy from drying out.

Serve with fried or mashed potatoes, broccoli and hot biscuits.

VENISON WITH ROGERS' DUMPLINGS

Venison from elk, moose or deer may be used in this recipe. It's a novel way of preparing stew meat, as well as a tasty one.

2 pounds stew meat cut into one-inch cubes	1 tablespoon Worcestershire sauce
3 tablespoons bacon fat or cooking oil	2 tablespoons dried onion flakes
1 teaspoon salt	Hot water
1 teaspoon pepper	

Salt and pepper the meat, and sauté in bacon fat or cooking oil until well browned. Add onion flakes and Worcestershire sauce and cook for one minute, stirring constantly. Add boiling water to cover and simmer until the meat is tender. This will take approximately one hour. Make dumplings (see recipe for Rogers' dumplings on page 141) and cook according to directions.

Serve with green beans and banana nut salad, followed by chocolate pie as dessert.

This should serve four hearty eaters.

VENISON RIBS, POLYNESIAN STYLE

I would venture to say that fifty per cent of all hunters discard the rib cage when they process a deer. If they only knew how delicious the ribs can be when properly prepared, they would never do such a thing again. Here is a fine way of serving them.

2 pounds venison ribs cut to serving size	½ cup catsup
⅔ cup dark brown sugar	¼ cup finely chopped onion
2 tablespoons corn starch	2 tablespoons soy sauce
2 teaspoons dry mustard	Salt
⅔ cup vinegar	Pepper
1 cup crushed pineapple	Cooking oil

Salt and pepper ribs and brown them in a small amount of cooking oil, making sure they are browned on both sides. Arrange them in a single layer in a shallow baking dish, with the meaty side down, in such a way that they will hold the sauce on top instead of letting it collect in the bottom.

To make the sauce, place remaining ingredients in a saucepan, add half a cup of water and cook over medium heat, stirring constantly, until the mixture is glossy and has begun to thicken. This will take approximately fifteen minutes. Pour half of this sauce on top of the ribs, and place the baking dish in a preheated oven at 325 degrees for forty-five minutes. Turn the ribs, pour on the remaining sauce and bake at the same temperature for forty-five minutes longer.

Begin the meal with a grapefruit appetizer (see page 137). With the ribs, serve baked yams and cauliflower au gratin. For dessert we suggest butterscotch pudding.

This recipe will serve two or three people.

VENISON RIBS WITH NOODLES

This is another way of serving one of our favorite portions of venison, and one that is very little trouble.

3 pounds venison ribs cut to serving size	1 two-ounce can mushrooms
3 tablespoons bacon fat	1 six-ounce package noodles
1 tablespoon chopped onion	Salt
¼ teaspoon Worcestershire sauce	Pepper

Salt and pepper the ribs and cook in a skillet containing bacon fat until brown on all sides. Add onions and Worcestershire sauce, and cook for two minutes. Then add enough water to cover, and simmer until the meat is tender. Add mushrooms and noodles and cook ten minutes more, or until noodles are tender.

Serve with string beans and sliced tomatoes, followed by chocolate cake for dessert.

VENISON RIBS AND ROGERS' DUMPLINGS

3 pounds venison ribs	¼ teaspoon Worcestershire
3 tablespoons bacon fat	sauce
1 medium onion	Salt
¼ teaspoon marjoram	Pepper
¼ teaspoon oregano	Flour
	Hot water

Melt bacon fat in a heavy skillet or deep kettle. Salt, pepper and flour the ribs and brown them in bacon fat. Add chopped onion, Worcestershire sauce, marjoram and oregano. Simmer for three minutes, then cover the meat with hot water. Turn the fire low, cover with a tight-fitting lid and simmer approximately one and a half hours.

Make Rogers' dumplings (see page 141; half the recipe will be sufficient) and cook according to directions.

Serve with a green vegetable and a salad of pineapple and grated cheese, followed by blueberry pie for dessert.

This recipe will feed four people.

VENISON RIBS SUPERB

After numerous experiments we have found this recipe to be what we were striving for. It serves four people.

Venison ribs cut to a length of four or five inches, allowing about five inches per person (more for hearty eaters)	1 medium-size green pepper, seeds removed, chopped fine
	2 cloves garlic
2 tablespoons bacon fat or cooking oil	1 teaspoon Worcestershire sauce
3 small cans tomato sauce	Salt
1 large onion	Pepper
	Flour

Salt and pepper the ribs to taste and dust thoroughly with flour. Put bacon fat or cooking oil in a heavy skillet, place ribs in skillet and brown on both sides. When brown, add onion and garlic, but keep stirring until onion browns. Add Worcestershire sauce, tomato sauce and green pepper. Add sufficient water to cover the ribs and let simmer for one hour, or until liquid has cooked down to a medium sauce.

Serve with steamed browned rice and green beans. For dessert, try apple pie with milk or cream or, if you prefer, heat pie with a slice of cheese on it.

VENISON SHANK À LA MONTANA

Most hunters cut the meat off the shank and either grind it or use it as stew meat. But contrary to what many of them suppose, the meat is tender and has a rich, nutty flavor. Here is a different method of cooking the shank, which we like very much. We use the shank of the deer or antelope for this dish, serving one shank per person.

4 deer or antelope shanks	¼ teaspoon crushed rosemary
2 tablespoons bacon fat or	leaves
cooking oil	¼ teaspoon thyme
1 large onion	¼ cup brown sugar
1 small can tomato sauce	Salt
½ cup cooking sherry	Pepper
	Flour

Flour, salt and pepper the shanks, and place with bacon fat or cooking oil in a deep skillet or Dutch oven and brown lightly over medium heat. Meanwhile, place in another utensil the chopped onion, tomato sauce, water, cooking sherry, rosemary, thyme and brown sugar. After the meat has cooked for about ten minutes, pour the sauce over it, cover and simmer for one and a half or two hours, depending upon the size of the shank.

If necessary, add a little water so that the sauce completely covers the meat at the beginning of the cooking process; but do not add any water while it is cooking.

Serve with fluffy white rice or mashed potatoes, spinach and spiced figs. Follow with a light dessert.

This recipe should serve four hungry people.

VENISON WITH ANJOU PEARS

2 serving pieces venison,	¾ cup dark brown sugar
approximately one inch thick	¼ cup soy sauce
1 tablespoon cooking oil	½ teaspoon ginger
2 thin slices lemon	¾ cup water
4 slices onion, medium thin	Salt
1 Anjou pear, halved and cored	Pepper

Salt and pepper the venison and lightly brown it in cooking oil. Then place a slice of lemon and two slices of onion on top of the meat. Arrange pear halves in the skillet next to the meat, cut side down. Mix the remaining ingredients, pour over the meat and pears, cover and simmer fifteen minutes. Turn the pears and simmer for another fifteen minutes, basting the meat occasionally.

Serve with fluffy steamed rice, a green salad and hard rolls. Dessert might be peach cobbler with cream.

The recipe serves two people.

RIGATONI STUFFED WITH VENISON

Here is a colorful and tasty dish that will bring compliments from both family and guests whenever you serve it. Though it is a little complicated to prepare, you will find the results well worth the effort.

2 pounds ground venison (be sure to grind some beef suet with the meat)
1 teaspoon crushed rosemary leaves
¼ teaspoon thyme
¼ teaspoon nutmeg
¼ teaspoon marjoram
1 clove garlic, crushed
1 teaspoon dried shredded green onions

1 tablespoon dried onion flakes, or one small chopped onion
Salt
Pepper
2 small cans tomato sauce
¼ pound Longhorn or Cheddar cheese

Mix all the ingredients in a large bowl and let them stand while you prepare the rigatoni.

Cook one-half pound of rigatoni according to the directions on the package. Set aside and allow to cool. After the rigatoni has cooled, stuff it with the meat mixture. This is the time-consuming part of the recipe. Arrange the stuffed rigatoni in layers in a baking dish measuring approximately 8" x 12" x 3". Cover with thin slices of Longhorn or Cheddar cheese. Dilute two small cans of tomato sauce with equal parts of water and pour on top. Place in a preheated oven at 350 degrees for fifteen minutes, then lower the temperature to 275 degrees and bake for thirty minutes more.

Serve with Caesar salad, hard French bread or rolls or garlic bread, and a good red wine. For dessert, Key lime pie is an excellent choice.

The recipe serves four or more.

VENISON SALISBURY STEAK SUPREME

There are many appetizing ways of using ground venison, and we think you will find this one of the best. Properly prepared ground venison is so far superior to the usual "ground meat" that there is no comparison. But be sure you grind some beef suet with your venison, so that it will not be dry.

¾ pound ground venison per person (if you are cooking for hearty eaters)
1 chopped onion (optional)

3 thin slices of Longhorn or Cheddar cheese per steak
Salt
Pepper

Mix the chopped onion into the ground venison and place in a lightly greased skillet. Cook until lightly brown, turn and add salt and pepper to taste. Place cheese slices on the meat and cook until the cheese is soft or melted.

Serve with baked potatoes or French fries and a tossed green salad with your choice of dressing, followed by pie or cobbler for dessert.

SUPER DELUXE VENISON CHEESEBURGERS

This is something different in the way of burgers. Though it takes time to cook, it is worth the wait.

3 pounds ground venison, makes a dozen average-sized burgers
Sandwich buns
1 onion, sliced thin
Dill pickles
Longhorn or Cheddar cheese

Thyme
Rosemary
Ketchup (optional)
Mustard (optional)
Salt
Pepper

Cut buns in half and spread both halves liberally with butter or margarine. On the bottom half place a venison patty, cover with cheese, dill pickle, salt and pepper to taste, and sprinkle lightly with rosemary and thyme. Wrap each bun individually in aluminum foil, sealing securely. Place in oven pre-heated to 350 degrees and bake approximately forty-five minutes.

Remove, unwrap foil and add onion, mustard, or ketchup as desired. Allow at least two sandwiches per person and possibly three or more for hearty eaters.

VENISON MEATBALLS AND SPAGHETTI

In this recipe you may use whatever kind of venison you have—deer, elk, moose or antelope.

Meatballs

1 pound ground venison, to which you have added a small amount of beef suet
¼ medium onion, ground
1 teaspoon salt
¼ teaspoon pepper
1 teaspoon marjoram
¼ teaspoon thyme
½ teaspoon garlic powder
1 egg

Mix all these ingredients thoroughly, form into sixteen meat balls, and let them stand while you make the following sauce.

Sauce

1 pound can solid pack tomatoes
1 eight-ounce can tomato sauce
¼ cup minced onion
2 cloves garlic, crushed
1 teaspoon salt
1 tablespoon vegetable oil
¼ teaspoon ground cloves
1 teaspoon sage
¼ teaspoon pepper
1 cup water
¼ teaspoon thyme

Thoroughly mix all the sauce ingredients in a large kettle and bring to a simmer. After approximately fifteen minutes, add twelve of the meat balls, which have been browned in a heavy skillet with a small amount of cooking oil. Crumble the four remaining balls, and add a little water to loosen the residue in the bottom of the skillet. Pour the crumbled meat and residue into the kettle with the sauce and meat balls, cover and simmer for about two hours. If the sauce is too thin, make a small amount of flour paste, add to the sauce, and simmer until the desired thickness is attained.

Cook a twelve-ounce package of spaghetti according to directions, place on a large platter and cover with sauce and meat balls. Sprinkle with Parmesan cheese if desired.

Serve with a tossed green salad with Italian oil dressing, hard rolls or bread sticks, and a light red wine.

The recipe serves four.

PEPPERS STUFFED WITH VENISON

Among the many ways of using ground venison, we find this one excellent. If you have processed your own venison you will know what is in it, and that it doesn't consist of meat that could not be sold in any other way.

4 green peppers
1½ pounds ground venison
   (deer, elk or moose)
1 large potato, peeled and
   grated
1 medium onion, grated

½ teaspoon (dried green
   onion)
1 small can tomato sauce
4 thin slices Longhorn or
   Cheddar cheese
½ teaspoon salt
½ teaspoon pepper

Cut around the stem of the pepper, remove the seeds and parboil for ten minutes or until tender. Remove from the pot, drain and set aside to cool. Combine the meat, potatoes, onions, salt and pepper in a mixing bowl and blend thoroughly. Fill peppers with the mixture and place them in a lightly oiled baking dish in such a manner that they will remain upright. Place a slice of cheese over each pepper. Pour over all the tomato sauce, which has been diluted with equal parts of water.

Place in a preheated oven at 350 degrees and bake for one hour. If the peppers begin to look dry, add a little water.

Serve with at least one green vegetable, plus potatoes or rice. For dessert a light custard pudding would be suitable.

This recipe will serve four.

VENISON MEAT LOAF

Here is another appetizing way to use ground venison, and any that is left over will make delicious sandwiches the next day.

2½ pounds ground venison, with beef suet	1 teaspoon Worcestershire sauce
¼ cup canned milk	Salt
1 clove garlic, minced	Pepper
1 large onion, grated	

Place the ingredients in a large mixing bowl and blend thoroughly. Then transfer to a well-oiled baking dish and let it sit in a cool place for about thirty minutes so that the meat will absorb the seasoning. Bake in a preheated oven at 350 degrees for one hour. If you wish, lay two or three slices of bacon over the loaf before putting it into the oven.

We cook vegetables to go with this meal as follows: Place potatoes, carrots and onions in the center of a piece of aluminum foil. Salt and pepper, and add two or three pats of butter or margarine, and approximately one-fourth cup of water. Using a drugstore wrap, seal aluminum securely and place in the oven to cook along with the meat loaf. When the meat is done, the vegetables will also be ready.

This recipe should serve four hungry people. For dessert, give them pie or ice cream.

VENISON MINCEMEAT

Few sportsmen ever think of making mincemeat from their venison. You can use some of the choice stewing pieces, or, if you prefer, you may take the meat from the neck or some other portion of the deer. Either way you will be happy with the results.

3 pounds venison, boiled until tender and chopped fine or shredded (be sure to save the broth)	24 medium-sized apples, peeled and chopped fine
	1 tablespoon salt
	3 tablespoons cinnamon
2 pounds seedless raisins	1 teaspoon nutmeg
1 pound beef suet, chopped fine, and with membrane removed	2 cups vinegar
	5 pounds brown sugar
	2 cups meat broth
	1 teaspoon ground cloves

Place venison, suet, apples and broth in a kettle and cook until the apples are tender. Add the remaining ingredients and simmer fifteen minutes. Seal in hot sterilized jars. This recipe will make about fifteen pints.

Mincemeat is better after aging several months, better still after at least a year. When you serve your guests a game dinner topped off with venison mincemeat, you can expect nothing but the most favorable comment.

VENISON MINCEMEAT PIE

1 pint venison mincemeat
1 cup pineapple or orange
  juice

1 small jar citron (optional)
1 cup cooking sherry
Pastry crust for two eight-inch
  pies

Place mincemeat, juice, citron and sherry in a small kettle, and heat over a low flame for about ten minutes, stirring occasionally to keep from burning. If the mixture is too thin, add one or two teaspoons of tapioca—but do this only if necessary. Remove the mixture from the fire and let it cool.

Roll out pastry for a bottom crust and fill with mincemeat. Cover with lattice work or a full cover as for any two-crust pie. Bake at 400 degrees for ten minutes, then at 350 degrees for forty to fifty minutes.

Thin slices of Cheddar or Longhorn cheese placed on this pie while it is hot are delicious; or a good rum sauce may be poured over it.

VENISON LIVER FRIED IN DEEP FAT

This is a unique way of preparing venison liver, and one of which we are especially fond. The result is well done but still juicy and tasty.

1 pound venison liver cut into
  one-inch cubes
2 small onions, thinly sliced

2 sprigs parsley
Salt
Pepper

Sprinkle the liver with salt and pepper. Cover it with onion and parsley, and let stand for two hours. Fry in deep fat at 390 degrees for one minute. Drain and place on a serving platter; garnish with lemon slices and parsley.

Sweet corn and string beans are a good accompaniment, with peach cobbler for dessert.

This should serve four persons.

VENISON LIVER AND ONIONS

Properly cooked, venison liver is far superior to baby beef liver. For best results, do not slice it too thin, and do not overcook it as so many people do, since that will make it tough and tasteless. This recipe will serve four.

Allow two or three pieces of liver per person
1 large onion
8 to 10 slices of bacon

Salt
Pepper
Flour

Let the liver stand in a brine solution for approximately thirty minutes. Remove, rinse in cold water and place in a pan of boiling water to blanch; then blot it dry. Fry the bacon and remove it from the skillet as it becomes crisp. Sprinkle the liver with salt and pepper, roll it in flour and drop it into the bacon fat, heated to approximately 275 degrees. Cover the skillet, and cook until slightly brown. Turn the liver, and cover it with thinly sliced onions. When the liver is browned and the onions are tender, remove them from the skillet to a hot platter. Garnish with strips of crisp bacon and parsley.

Serve with cream style corn, spinach and a salad of grated carrots and cabbage with dressing, followed by pineapple upside-down cake.

SMOTHERED VENISON LIVER

6 to 10 slices liver
1 tablespoon bacon fat
1 can stewed tomatoes
½ canful of water
¼ teaspoon celery salt
1 teaspoon dried shredded green onion
6 green onions, sliced or chopped fine

¼ teaspoonful of thyme
¼ teaspoonful of basil, crushed
10 thinly sliced rings of green pepper
Salt
Pepper
Flour

Heat the bacon fat in a heavy skillet. Salt, pepper and flour the liver and brown it in the fat. Turn just once. When it is lightly browned on both sides, add remaining ingredients and simmer uncovered about an hour. Stir occasionally so that it doesn't burn.

Serve with corn on the cob, tossed green salad and hot rolls.

For desert, serve sliced fresh peaches and cream.

This recipe will serve three or four.

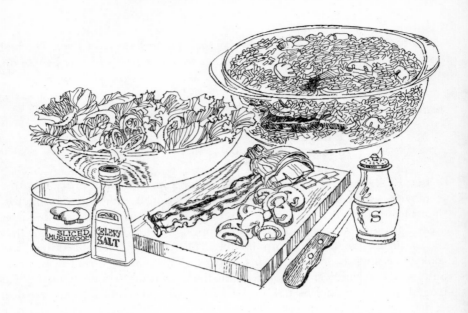

VENISON LIVER WITH RICE AND BACON

1 or 2 pieces liver, one inch thick, per serving	5 slices bacon
½ cup marsh or wild rice	1 small onion, chopped
1 two-ounce can mushroom stems and pieces	½ teaspoon salt
	¼ teaspoon celery salt
	Pepper

Place the rice in a stew pot; add two cups of water and the half teaspoon of salt. Bring to a rapid boil, reduce heat and simmer for twenty minutes. Add mushrooms, onion and celery salt, cover and simmer for twenty minutes more.

Fry bacon crisp and crumble it. Pour off most of the grease, and sear liver thoroughly on both sides in what remains in the skillet. Add the crumbled bacon to the rice mixture, stirring gently. Place a thin layer of the rice in a casserole, then a layer of liver, then the rest of the rice. Bake in a preheated oven at 400 degrees for ten minutes; then reduce to 300 degrees and cook for twenty minutes more.

Serve with a tossed green salad.

The recipe will serve two.

BAKED VENISON LIVER

Another tasty way of preparing venison liver. Try it for a change some evening.

1½ pounds venison liver	⅛ teaspoon thyme
7 strips bacon	2 eggs
1 large onion, chopped fine	1 cup milk
1 dozen Ritz or Hi-Ho crackers	Salt
⅛ teaspoon marjoram	Pepper

Cover the liver with water, and boil until firm enough to slice into thin pieces. Cut three slices of bacon into small pieces and sauté. Remove from fire, add chopped onions, and mix thoroughly.

In a casserole place a thin layer of bacon and onion mixture, using approximately a third of the total amount. On top of this place two layers of thinly sliced liver, and cover with bacon and onion mixture, using approximately half the remaining amount. Crush six crackers and spread the crumbs evenly over the top. Add the remainder of the sliced liver and cover it with the balance of the onion and bacon mixture. Crush six more crackers and spread the crumbs over the top. Beat the eggs lightly, add the milk and mix thoroughly. Sprinkle majoram, thyme, salt and pepper over the contents of the casserole, and pour in the eggs and milk. Finally, lay the four remaining strips of bacon on top, place the casserole in a preheated oven at 325 degrees, and bake for one hour.

Serve with buttered asparagus tips and spaghetti in a tomato-cheese sauce.

For dessert we suggest Key lime pie.

This recipe should serve four hearty eaters.

BAKED VENISON HEART

Many prefer baking to any other method of preparing the heart. This is our favorite way of baking it.

1 venison heart	Salt
½ cup canned applesauce	Pepper
1 teaspoon oregano	

Boil the heart in salted water until tender. Remove it from the water and cut it into quarters. To stuff it, prepare whatever dressing you prefer, using white bread or corn bread. Add to it the applesauce and oregano.

Spread a layer of the dressing in a baking dish, place on it the quartered heart, and cover with the remainder of the dressing. Cover the dish and bake in a 350-degree oven for forty-five minutes.

Serve with a green salad and green string beans, followed by a dessert of pie or custard.

BOILED VENISON HEART

We find boiled venison heart an excellent sandwich meat similar to boiled tongue.

1 venison heart cut in half lengthwise	2 bay leaves
½ teaspoon salt	¼ teaspoon pepper
½ teaspoon marjoram	Dash nutmeg

Place two cups of water in a stew pot with seasonings, and boil five minutes to extract the flavor. Add the heart, cover and simmer until tender. This should take approximately forty-five minutes.

Remove from the flame and leave the heart to cool in the liquid, further absorbing the flavor of the herbs and spices. When cool, transfer to a dish and add a small amount of the liquid from the pot to keep the meat from drying out. Keep in the refrigerator until ready for use. Slice thin and serve on rye bread with horseradish or mustard. This makes a wonderful sandwich, delicious for between-meal snacks.

CORNED VENISON

There is no better meal than a good New England boiled dinner using corned venison, which in my opinion is far superior to corned beef. For the latter, most packing houses use the cheaper and tougher cuts, such as the brisket, thereby getting a much higher price for the otherwise undesirable parts. For corned venison we use only choice cuts, usually the ham or shoulder blade of the deer. From each ham, as you bone it, you will be able to get three good pieces of meat by separating the muscular segments. Cut these three segments from the bone, being sure to remove all the fat and also the glands between them. When we corn the blade we also cut the meat off the bone, using the same caution as for the hams.

Use a glass or crockery jar with a capacity of at least two gallons; a three-gallon one is preferable. Use a box of Morton's Tender Quick, following the directions on the box. Though we have tried other recipes, we find this one of the simplest and easiest. The meat must be kept completely submerged for at least two weeks, and the temperature should not exceed 38 degrees. Upon removing meat from the pickling jar, rinse it thoroughly in clear, cool water. Cook it according to the recipe that follows.

You should be able to corn enough venison at a time for three or four meals. What you don't cook immediately can be placed in a plastic bag and frozen for future use. In cooking, it will take on a deep red color, and properly prepared it makes the best of eating.

VENISON NEW ENGLAND BOILED DINNER

2 pounds corned venison	½ teaspoon pepper
2 strips beef suet	4 potatoes
2 bay leaves	4 carrots
1 teaspoon dried basil leaves	1 medium-sized head cabbage
4 medium-sized or small onions, left whole	

Rinse the venison thoroughly to remove the salt left by the corning process. Slit the meat with a sharp knife, place the strips of beef suet in the slits, and tie securely with butchers' twine. Cover with cold water, bring to a boil and simmer for four or five minutes. Pour off the liquid and cover again with cold water. Add bay leaves, onions, pepper and basil leaves. Cook over a low fire for six hours at a slow simmer, not a vigorous boil. *This is very important. Corned venison cooked too fast will be tough.*

Now add the potatoes and carrots, and cook until they are almost done. During the last ten or twelve minutes of cooking, cut the cabbage into wedges and add to the pot. It shouldn't take more than ten or twelve minutes to cook the cabbage.

Serve with hot cornbread muffins or cornbread sticks, or if you prefer, light bread or rolls. For dessert we suggest a good pan pudding.

JERKED VENISON

Making jerked venison, or jerky, isn't the complicated job you might think. All you need is salt, pepper, venison and—most important—a *sharp knife.*

The ham of the deer is the easiest part to slice, so we generally use that. Remember to slice *with the grain,* not crosswise. As you slice, place the slabs on a board or table. Be sure all the fat is removed, leaving only the lean red meat. Salt and pepper both sides very generously and hang on a wire or string, or place the meat on racks in such a manner that air can circulate freely around it. Hang on a screened porch if possible, or in some place where flies can't get to it.

With low humidity, and a temperature of 55 to 70 degrees, the meat should be cured in about forty-eight hours. Remove and place in a porous cloth bag, and let it continue to hang as you use it. The larger, thicker pieces, which may need a little longer, will continue to cure in the bag.

When you go to the wood or stream, cram your pockets full of this tasty and nutritious food. Jerked meat will keep almost indefinitely, and you'll understand why it's so expensive to buy.

SMOKED VENISON JERKY

Many outdoorsmen keep some sort of smoker around the house for curing various sorts of game. It's easy to build one, and if you want to make some jerky with a genuine smoked flavor, try this simple method.

Slice meat with the grain, being sure all fat has been trimmed away, and salt generously on both sides. Place in smoker and use hardwood for fuel, preferably hickory, pecan or some nut wood if available. (Hickory chips can be purchased at many sporting goods stores.) Build a low fire and try to keep it smoldering to create smoke. Do not let it get too hot; that will make the jerky dry and brittle instead of chewy, as it should be.

Leave the meat in the smoker four to six hours to absorb the flavor; then remove and hang on a wire to complete the curing. You will find this a highly flavorsome jerky, and quite unlike the kind for sale in stores and delicatessens.

CREAMED JERKY ON TOAST

½ cup coarsely ground jerked venison
½ cup water
3 tablespoons margarine or butter

2 rounded tablespoons flour
2 cups milk, or enough to make a medium thick sauce
Bread for toast

Place the ground meat in a small stew pot with the water and bring to a boil. Remove from the fire and let it stand for one hour. Melt the butter or margarine in a skillet and add flour, mixing well to form a smooth paste. Remove the skillet from the fire and add the milk, stirring constantly. When the mixture is smooth, return to the fire, continuing to stir and adding just enough milk to make a medium thick sauce.

At this point add the contents of the stew pot, mix thoroughly and simmer for about ten minutes, stirring occasionally. Toast and butter the bread and spoon the creamed meat over it, sprinkle lightly with parsley flakes and serve piping hot.

This makes a delicious lunch. A little smoked jerky mixed with the sun-cured meat will add to the flavor.

Pronghorn Antelope

The pronghorn antelope is a bundle of nervous energy, and one of the most graceful, alert and colorful animals of the Western plains. It is also the speediest of them all. Some people disrespectfully refer to it as the "prairie goat." Hunting this animal in a sportsmanlike manner is a thrilling and satisfying adventure.

It is strictly a plains animal, and doesn't depend upon brush and timber for concealment as do the deer and elk. You will find pronghorn antelope in the vast open spaces, where with their telescopic vision—said to equal that of a man using eight-power binoculars—they can detect the slightest movement at uncanny distances. When feeding or resting, they always have a sentry on duty to warn them in case of danger.

Skill and patience are needed to stalk the wary pronghorn, for at times it has an exasperating way of seeming to know the exact range of your gun. A good stalk and a clean kill at a long distance will do much to boost your ego.

Contrary to what is sometimes said, properly field dressed and cared for, the meat of the antelope is one of the finest pieces of venison. It is fine-textured and somewhat lighter in color than deer. I have seen unsportsmanlike hunters chase the antelope with a pickup or car, then shoot it and wonder why the meat was unpalatable. The finest beef killed under such conditions would be unfit for eating.

BAKED KABOB OF ANTELOPE

Shiskebab, a favorite dish for the barbecue pit, of course means cubes of meat, marinated and cooked with onions, tomatoes and other vegetables. Baked kabob, a very similar dish and just as tasty, can be done indoors. It is a whole meal within itself.

20 pieces antelope, cut into cubes approximately two inches square	Salt Pepper Mace
1 tablespoon cooking oil	Nutmeg
2 medium-sized onions	Thyme
1 green pepper	Worcestershire sauce
1 small can sliced pineapple	

Place cooking oil in skillet and sear the meat. Add a few drops of Worcestershire sauce during the process. Remove the meat from the flame and let it cool. Shape a piece of aluminum foil to fit the baking dish you plan to use, making sure to have it large enough so that it can be folded and sealed after placing the ingredients in it.

In the center of the foil in its baking dish, alternate a piece of meat with a slice of onion and a slice of pepper, to form a circle around the inside of the baking dish.

By the time all three ingredients have been used up, the bottom of the dish should be solidly covered. Place the pineapple on top and sprinkle with salt, pepper, mace, nutmeg and thyme. Pour the pineapple juice from the can into the skillet previously used to sear the meat, place it over a low flame and stir constantly until you have thoroughly mixed the juice with the residue of oil and meat that is left in the skillet. Pour this mixture over the contents of the baking dish, and use a drugstore wrap to seal the aluminum foil. Place in a preheated oven at 350 degrees for one hour.

This will feed two hungry people. A side dish of some green vegetable may be served if desired.

ANTELOPE CHOPS, PAN FRIED

2 chops per person   Salt
Flour   Pepper
Cooking oil

Salt and pepper the chops and dust lightly with flour. Place heavy skillet over flame until medium hot, and pour in just enough cooking oil to barely cover the bottom. Place chops in skillet, cover and cook five to eight minutes. Remove cover, turn chops and cook five minutes more. By now they should be pink, juicy and tender. Do not overcook or use too hot a fire, or the meat will be tough and dry.

Serve with hominy fried in a small amount of bacon fat, buttered summer squash, and a salad of sliced tomatoes, followed by strawberry shortcake for dessert.

ROAST BLADE OF DEER OR ANTELOPE

Since we like a good roast, we never cut the blade into steaks as some hunters do. The blade of a deer or antelope is about the best roast you will find on either of these animals—tender, juicy and very flavorsome.

5 pounds or one whole blade of   Pepper
  an average-sized deer or   Garlic salt
  antelope   2 tablespoons Worcestershire
Salt   sauce

Be sure to remove any surplus fat from the meat. Cover it with bacon fat, or if none is available place two or three strips of bacon over the roast. Salt and pepper, using a little garlic salt, and smear two tablespoons of Worcestershire sauce on the meat.

Place the roast on a double thickness of aluminum foil, and using the drugstore wrap seal it completely. Set this in a shallow pan, so that in the event of a broken seal or a puncture in the foil, the juices will be caught. Place in the oven, set the temperature at 350 degrees, and roast for three and a half hours. For a roast that is frozen when you start to cook, set the oven at 400 degrees for the first hour, then reduce to 350.

Serve with potatoes au gratin, spinach and pickled beets, followed by custard pudding for dessert.

This recipe should serve four hearty eaters.

ROAST LEG OF ANTELOPE

A well-cared-for leg of antelope is comparable if not superior to a choice leg of lamb. It doesn't need a lot of fancy sauces to make it one of the most succulent roasts you ever ate. This simple recipe lets you retain the distinct, delicate flavor of this tasty animal.

4–5 pounds leg of antelope, boned (if you can't do this, get your butcher to do it for you)	Pepper
	4 slices beef suet, approximately ½ inch thick and 2 or 3 inches square
Salt	

Rub salt and pepper into the roast on all sides and place on a rack in the roasting pan. Lay on the slices of suet. Roast in a preheated oven at 350 degrees for two hours for medium rare, longer for well done; but do not overcook. Place potatoes around meat and bake for one hour before meat is done. Test with a fork.

Serve with green peas, mint jelly or spiced crabapples, and a grapefruit and avocado salad.

BRAISED SIRLOIN TIP OF ANTELOPE

Braised sirloin tips of beef make an excellent dish. You will find the same cut of the antelope equally appetizing.

1 pound antelope sirloin tips	3 carrots cut into one-inch pieces
1 clove garlic, minced	Salt
1 cup solid pack tomatoes	Pepper
1 tablespoon bacon fat	Flour
2 medium-sized potatoes	
1 large onion, cut into quarters	

Salt, pepper and flour the tips and brown in the bacon fat over a medium fire. When the meat is brown, cover with boiling water and add garlic, tomatoes and onions. Simmer forty-five minutes to one hour. Add potatoes and carrots, and cook until tender, or approximately thirty-five minutes. Remove the vegetables from the pot and thicken the liquid with two tablespoons of flour dissolved in a cup of water.

Serve with French bread or hard rolls and a green salad, followed by a dessert of fruit or jello.

This will serve two people.

ANTELOPE AND NAVY BEAN CASSEROLE

1 pound antelope round steak	1 tablespoon bacon fat
1 fifteen-ounce can navy beans	Garlic powder
1 fourteen-ounce can stewed tomatoes	Salt
½ medium-sized onion, sliced and separated into rings	Pepper

Season the antelope round with salt, papper and garlic salt, and brown in a heavy skillet over a medium fire. Place the navy beans in the bottom of a casserole, lay the browned meat over them, and cover with stewed tomatoes. Place the onion rings on top and bake in a preheated oven at 350 degrees for forty-five minutes, then reduce to 250 degrees for thirty minutes more.

Serve with buttered beets and a green salad, followed by a dessert of chocolate cake.

This will serve two persons.

ANTELOPE CURRY

I am especially fond of lamb curry, and we find this dish prepared with choice antelope stew is equally good.

2 pounds antelope stew meat cut into bite-sized cubes	⅓ cup finely chopped sweet onion
4 tablespoons butter or margarine	2 teaspoons curry powder (more if desired)
¾ cup finely chopped tart apples	¾ teaspoon salt
	1 cup quick-cooking rice
	4 tablespoons chutney

Sear meat cubes in a heavy skillet until lightly brown. Cover with water and simmer until tender (a little over an hour). Remove, but save the broth; if there is not a full quart, add water. Place apples and onion in the skillet with butter and cook until tender. Mix salt and curry powder, stir into onion and apple mixture, and cook over a low fire for about fifteen minutes. Gradually pour in the broth, stirring constantly until the mixture thickens, then simmer for approximately fifteen minutes, stirring occasionally. Add chutney to antelope and heat well before serving. Spoon over precooked rice.

This makes four liberal servings.

ANTELOPE STEW

Since the antelope is a small animal, you won't have much meat for stew. This makes a good one.

2 pounds antelope meat cut into 2-inch cubes	1 tablespoon Worcestershire sauce
½ teaspoon celery seed	5 potatoes, medium size
¼ teaspoon dried basil leaves	5 turnips, medium size
¼ teaspoon cumin seed	5 carrots
1 can solid pack tomatoes	1 package frozen okra, or one-half pound fresh if available
1 large onion, chopped	
2 tablespoons bacon fat or cooking oil	Salt
	Pepper

Salt, pepper and flour meat and brown in bacon fat or oil. Add onion and Worcestershire sauce, and stir until onion is light brown. Cover meat with hot water, add tomatoes and simmer one hour. Add celery seed and basil leaves. Simmer for thirty minutes, then add potatoes, carrots and turnips. When nearly done, add okra and continue to cook until meat is tender.

Serve with cornbread sticks or muffins and a salad of lemon jello with crushed pineapple and cottage cheese, with gooseberry pie for dessert.

This will serve three or four persons.

GROUND ANTELOPE WITH POTATO PANCAKE

An unusual way of using ground antelope.

1 pound ground antelope meat	1 small can mushroom buttons
1 package potato pancake mix	1 teaspoon Tabasco sauce
1 medium onion, chopped fine	1 cup shredded Cheddar or Longhorn cheese
1 cup cooked long-grain or wild rice	

Prepare potato pancake mix as directed on the box. Add half of the chopped onion to the batter, and let it stand fifteen minutes. Do not stir again. Cook potato cakes, making them about five inches in diameter. Remove from the griddle and place on a towel. In a heavy skillet, brown the antelope meat in a small amount of bacon fat or cooking oil. Add the remaining onion,

Tabasco sauce and salt and pepper to taste. Cook slowly for about ten minutes. Remove from the fire and add the mushroom buttons and rice.

Place two tablespoons of meat on each pancake, roll and fasten with a toothpick. Arrange one layer deep in a baking dish, sprinkle with shredded cheese and place under the broiler until the cheese is melted; by then, the rolls will have heated all the way through.

Serve with a cooked, green or dried vegetable, and a dessert of apple pie.

This will serve two hearty eaters.

Elk

The elk is the largest round-horned deer, so powerful a brute that no ordinary fence will keep it out of your field or haystack.

Field dressed, more than one bull elk has weighed up to a thousand pounds or even over; but a more usual field-dressed weight is five or six hundred pounds.

In summer, and until the cold and snow drive them down, elk in the Rocky Mountain region range well above the timberline. You will find the wapiti one of the hardest of the deer family to hunt. Unless you are very lucky, you will have to hunt hard to get one at all. You will be amazed to discover how close you can be to one without even seeing it until it bolts, and within seconds it will have a large tree or a brushpile between you and it. Then all you will be able to see is a large rump disappearing among the trees.

Your first kill of so grand an animal is a thrill to be recounted many times, but to me each new kill of a large bull is as thrilling as the first one. It is the most prized kill in the West, and in flavor and texture the meat is nearer to beef than any other venison.

ELK RUMP ROAST

The rump roast of elk is one of the most flavorsome pieces on the elk, one you may look forward to with eager anticipation.

5 to 7 pounds elk rump roast   Garlic powder
Cooking oil or bacon drippings   Worcestershire sauce
Salt   Flour
Pepper

Trim all excess fat off the roast and completely cover it with bacon fat or cooking oil. Then sprinkle quite generously with salt and pepper and with a small amount of garlic powder. You may rub the roast with a clove of garlic if you prefer. Sprinkle or rub thoroughly with flour, and place in a roasting pan with the fleshiest side down. Dab generously with Worcestershire sauce, placing several drops in the bottom of the pan. Cover with a tight-fitting lid or aluminum foil, and bake in a preheated oven at 350 degrees for three and a half hours for medium well done meat, adding a little water from time to time to keep moist.

To make gravy when the meat is done, remove the roast and place the pan over a low flame. Add two cups of water and simmer until all the residue and meat drippings have been dissolved. Stir two teaspoons of flour into a cup of water, pour into the roasting pan and stir until the gravy begins to bubble. The consistency of the gravy is determined by the amount of flour used in proportion to the juice in pan.

Serve with mashed potatoes, green beans or peas, and a salad of tomatoes, cucumbers and onion rings in dill and vinegar. For dessert, serve home-made ice cream.

ELK RIB ROAST BARBECUE

For the man who likes outdoor cooking on a barbecue stand, we recommend this elk rib roast.

6 to 8 pounds rib roast from elk or moose Salt Pepper	Beef suet Open pit barbecue sauce (see recipe on page 144)

Wipe the roast with a damp cloth and cut it in such a manner that strips of beef suet can be inserted into the slits. Tie up the roast with copper wire, place on the spit rod and fasten the tines. Baste frequently with barbecue sauce. Place a piece of pecan or mesquite wood at each end of the roast, close enough to produce a good smoke that will literally envelop the meat during the entire cooking process, giving it a true smoke flavor. The time will depend on how close the roast is to the fire or bed of coals.

Serve with baked potatoes dressed in sour cream to which you have added a little horseradish, French bread, and tossed green salad with your favorite oil dressing.

ELK RIB ROAST

Properly handled at each stage from the kill to the dining table, this is the finest roast from the animal.

5 pounds elk rib roast Salt Pepper	Flour Beef suet

Since all the elk fat has been removed in the processing, at the time of cooking we replace it with beef suet. Rub salt, pepper and flour well into the meat on all sides. You may prefer, as some do, to use coarsely ground pepper. Cut slices of beef suet into long strips that can be draped over the meat and held in place with toothpicks. Place the meat in a roaster with a rack in the bottom, preheat the oven to 270 degrees and cook thirty minutes to the pound—or, if you use a meat thermometer, to 140 degrees for rare meat, 160 for medium, 170 for well done.

Serve with baked or mashed potatoes, green beans, and as a salad, asparagus vinaigrette with hard-boiled eggs. Dessert might be pie or cobbler.

ELK CHOPS, PAN FRIED

If you have been lucky enough to bring down a large elk, one chop per serving should be sufficient. From a smaller animal, you may need two per serving.

2 large elk chops (allowing one per serving)
2 tablespoons bacon fat or cooking oil
2 teaspoons Worcestershire sauce
1 teaspoon parsley flakes
Salt
Pepper

Season the chops with salt and pepper. Place a heavy skillet over the flame until medium hot, put in the chops, cover with an inverted pie plate, and cook from five to ten minutes. Remove the pie plate, turn the chops, add Worcestershire sauce and cook uncovered for five to ten minutes more. The additional time is dependent upon whether you like your meat rare, medium or well done. Remove the chops to a platter. Add a small amount of water to the skillet, loosening the residue and stirring as you add parsley flakes. Pour this sauce over the meat and potatoes.

Serve with mashed or baked potatoes, buttered asparagus tips, and a salad of lettuce wedges with your choice of dressing.

ELK OR MOOSE HASH

When you have leftovers from an elk or moose roast and don't plan to save them for tacos, try this delicious hash.

1 pound ground leftover roast of elk or moose
2 medium-sized potatoes
1 medium-sized onion
1 teaspoon oregano
½ teaspoon thyme
⅛ teaspoon cayenne pepper
1 strip bacon, cut in half
Salt
Pepper
1 cup water

Grind meat, potatoes and onion in meat grinder. Add all the remaining ingredients except the bacon and mix thoroughly. Place in a casserole that has been well greased with bacon fat, lay the two strips of bacon on top and bake in a 400-degree oven for one hour.

Serve with buttered beets, followed by lemon cake with sauce for dessert.

ELKBURGER COOKOUT

The elk is such a large animal that in the processing you will have a lot of meat suitable for grinding. To provide an evening of fun, invite your children's friends over sometime for an elkburger cookout. It will make a most favorable impression upon youngsters anywhere from six to sixty.

6 pounds elk, using some of your choice stew meat	¼ cup canned milk
¾ pound beef suet	Salt
2 eggs	Pepper

Grind the elk, using a medium blade, along with the beef suet. Add eggs and milk and mix thoroughly. Form patties to fit into wire hamburger cookers, place on a grill over charcoal and cook until done, turning as often as necessary. Have all the condiments on the table and let each guest build an elkburger to suit his taste. Have plenty of cold bottled drinks for the children, with ice cream for dessert. If you don't use wire hamburger cookers, you may add a little liquid smoke to the meat and cook it in a large skillet or griddle over charcoal.

ELK GROUND STEAK CASSEROLE

This is a tasty way to serve elk stew meat, ground up.

1 pound elk ground with beef suet	Salt
2 tablespoons chopped onion	Pepper

Mix the above, shape into three or four patties, and brown in a heavy skillet over medium heat. Set aside and make the following sauce:

1 one-pound can red kidney beans in barbecue sauce	½ teaspoon salt
½ cup water	½ teaspoon oregano
1 medium onion, chopped	1 teaspoon garlic powder
	1 teaspoon chili powder

Mix the ingredients and simmer for ten minutes. Pour into a casserole, place the meat patties on top, cover with Longhorn cheese and bake in a 325-degree oven for thirty minutes. May be served on split, warmed and buttered hamburger buns or on a platter with crackers. If you like, pickled chili peppers may be served as a condiment.

BOILED TONGUE OF ELK OR MOOSE

The elk and moose are both large animals, and the tongue of one is comparable to that of a beef. Properly prepared, it makes a delicious sandwich meat.

1 or 2 tongues of elk or moose	Salt
3 cloves	Pepper
2 bay leaves	

Using a fairly stiff brush, clean the tongue thoroughly under the warm-water tap. Place it in a stew pot and bring to a boil. Pour off the water and refill the pot. Add clove, bay leaves, salt and pepper, cover and simmer until the tongue is tender. At this point the skin should peel off very easily. If you wish, you may pierce the tongue with a knife point and·insert two or three cloves. Slice crosswise to serve.

Serve on rye bread with horseradish or mustard.

Moose

The moose is the largest member of the deer family, and a bull may weigh anywhere from a thousand to fifteen hundred pounds. The largest of all are the Alaskan moose, which may reach a shoulder height of from eighty to nearly a hundred inches, and weigh up to eighteen hundred pounds.

Unlike those of white-tailed deer or elk, the antlers of a moose are flat, with something of a palmetto shape, so that they are sometimes referred to as palms or fronds. The moose has a long, mulelike head with a large, overhanging upper lip, and is blackish brown in color. It is a very ungainly animal, with a shoulder much higher than the rump, a humped back and a neck so short that it must either wade into the water or kneel to get a drink. If the grass is very short, the moose will have to kneel to eat.

In summer you will usually find moose in lowland swamps, since their food at this time of the year consists mainly of pondweeds, lily pads and the tender young shoots of the willow.

The cow moose usually has a single calf after the first mating. But as with the mule deer, twins are not uncommon, and in a few instances a cow will give birth to triplets after the second or third mating. The newborn calves are not spotted or striped, but closely resemble their mother.

During the rutting season the bull is cantankerous and contrary if molested. More than one hunter has spent several hours on the limb of a tree waiting for an irate bull moose to leave. A friend of mine says the Montana moose are so smart that if one trees you, he will send a cow moose to find a beaver and have it cut the tree down for him! Nevertheless, you will find the moose easier to hunt and stalk than the elk, since it doesn't startle so easily. When you've made your kill, it is no use to tie a rope around the antlers and drag it home. To transport so huge an animal you will need heavy equipment, especially if you have made the kill in some inaccessible spot.

MOOSE RIB ROAST

The moose is so huge an animal that you will be able to get some exceptionally large roasts from it. A moose rib roast is comparable to one from a beef. Here is the way we prepare it.

5 pounds rib roast of moose   Salt
Beef suet   Pepper
1 clove garlic (optional)

If you elect to use the garlic, cut gashes in the roast and push slivers of garlic in quite deep. Don't over-season; the secret with garlic is to use just enough to make you wish there had been a little more. Rub salt and pepper very generously over the entire roast. Place strips of beef suet over the meat, and fix them in place with toothpicks. Place on a rack in the roaster and bake in a preheated over at 350 degrees for thirty minutes to the pound, or to a temperature of 140 degrees for rare, 150 for medium, 160 for well done.

With it serve baked potatoes dressed in sour cream and chives, green string beans, French bread and a crisp tossed salad with oil and vinegar dressing. A good Burgundy is perfect with this meal.

MOOSE RIBS WITH MUSHROOM SAUCE

Moose ribs, like those of beef, have a lot of meat on them. Any way you may prepare beef ribs can be used for moose. This is one of our favorites.

2 pounds moose short ribs   Salt
1 ten-and-a-half ounce can   Pepper
  mushroom soup   2 tablespoons minced onion
1 can mushroom stems and   Bacon grease
  pieces   Flour
1 cup water

Heat the bacon grease over a medium flame in a large, heavy skillet. Salt, pepper and flour the ribs and brown on all sides. Add minced onion, mix the mushroom soup with water until smooth, then add to the meat with the mushroom stems and pieces. Simmer until tender, or for approximately one hour.

Serve with mashed potatoes, turnip greens or spinach, and a jello salad. This will serve two persons.

MOOSE RIBS WITH BARBECUE SAUCE

This is another delicious way of preparing the rib portion of a moose. Elk ribs may also be used.

2 pounds moose or elk ribs
Salt
Pepper

Sauce:
1 eight-ounce can tomato sauce

1 can water (using tomato sauce can)
3 tablespoons Worcestershire sauce
1 teaspoon chili powder
1 medium onion, chopped
1 clove garlic, crushed

Mix all sauce ingredients thoroughly. Salt and pepper the ribs and place in a lightly oiled baking dish. Pour the sauce on top and bake approximately two hours in a 300-degree oven. Check occasionally, and if the meat seems to be drying out, turn down to 250 degrees.

Serve with fried hominy and Brussels sprouts, followed by lemon pie for dessert.

This will feed two hearty eaters.

SHORT RIBS OF MOOSE

Short ribs are my first choice whenever I find them on the menu in a restaurant, and I find moose short ribs equally good, or even better, since most of the fat has been trimmed off.

2 pounds short ribs of moose, cut into two- or three-inch lengths
2 tablespoons bacon fat or cooking oil

1 teaspoon Worcestershire sauce
Salt
Pepper
Flour
Hot water

Salt and pepper the ribs, roll them in flour, and brown in a heavy skillet with bacon fat or cooking oil. Add Worcestershire sauce. When thoroughly brown, place the ribs in a shallow baking dish and cover with hot water. Bake in a preheated oven at 350 degrees for an hour to an hour and a half. By then the meat should be tender, and the liquid will have cooked down to a thin gravy.

Serve with mashed potatoes or fluffy rice, Brussels sprouts, and a fruit salad.

This will serve three or four hungry persons.

MOOSE ROUND WITH SCALLOPED POTATOES

This is one of the best ways of cooking moose round steak—tender, juicy and luscious!

4 pieces moose round (two per serving), cut half an inch thick	1 medium-sized onion, sliced
	Salt
	Pepper
1 tablespoon bacon fat	Celery salt
3 medium-sized potatoes, sliced	1 cup water

Salt, pepper and lightly sprinkle the meat with celery salt. Heat the bacon fat in a heavy skillet over a medium fire, and sear or lightly brown on both sides. Remove the skillet from the fire and let it stand. Slice the potatoes into a casserole, place meat on top, and onion over all. Reheat the skillet and pour water into it to loosen the residue from the searing process. Pour this over the meat, cover with aluminum foil and bake in a preheated oven at 350 degrees for one and a half hours.

Accompany with green beans simplified (see recipe on page 138).

This will serve two hearty eaters.

MOOSE SALISBURY STEAK

¾ pound moose stew meat	¼ cup finely chopped onion
½ cup beef suet	Salt
1 egg	Pepper

Grind moose meat and beef suet just before they are to be used. Add the remaining ingredients and mix well. Divide into two portions pressed out to a thickness of about three-quarters of an inch. Place on a lightly greased, medium hot griddle or heavy skillet. Cook on one side for five to eight minutes, turn and cook five minutes more for a very tasty, juicy steak.

Serve with hashed brown or French-fried potatoes, and a good tossed green salad. For dessert we suggest strawberry shortcake and whipped cream.

This will serve two persons.

MOOSE STEW

When we make a stew, we treat it as a complete meal in itself. This recipe is one of our favorites.

2 pounds moose stew meat cut into bite-sized cubes	¼ teaspoon garlic powder
1 No. 303 can stewed tomatoes	½ teaspoon celery seed
4 carrots, cut into quarters	1 teaspoon parsley flakes
4 potatoes, cut into quarters	1 teaspoon Worcestershire sauce
2 medium-sized onions, cut in half	Bacon grease or cooking oil
1 green pepper, seeded and quartered	Salt
1 rutabaga or turnip, cut into quarters	Pepper
	Flour

Salt, pepper and flour the meat and brown it in bacon fat in a Dutch oven or heavy skillet. Add garlic, celery seed, parsley, Worcestershire sauce, pepper, tomatoes, onions and four cups of water. Cover and simmer for an hour and a half, then add carrots and rutabaga and cook fifteen minutes. Add potatoes and cook until the vegetables are done, or approximately thirty to forty-five minutes.

Serve with cornbread, French rolls or bread, and a tossed green salad with oil dressing.

MOOSE MEAT LOAF

1 pound moose meat, ground with beef suet	2 tablespoons finely chopped onion
8 Cheese Ritz crackers, crushed	1 small can tomato sauce
¼ teaspoon garlic salt	4 or 5 slices Cheddar or Longhorn cheese
1 egg	Salt
¼ cup evaporated egg	Pepper
¼ medium-sized green pepper, chopped	

Place all the ingredients in a bowl except the cheese and tomato sauce. Mix well and place in a small, well greased baking dish. Place sliced cheese over the ingredients and pour the tomato sauce on top. In a preheated oven at 350 degrees, bake forty-five minutes to one hour.

Serve with corn on the cob, and a salad of lemon jello with grated carrot and sliced stuffed green olives, followed by a dessert of custard pudding.

MOOSE IN ZUCCHINI BOATS

¾ pound ground moose meat	⅛ teaspoon thyme
4 zucchini squashes, average size	⅛ teaspoon marjoram
1 can Cheddar cheese soup	Small pinch garlic powder
1 egg	Salt
½ teaspoon Worcestershire sauce	Pepper

Wash the squash and boil for ten minutes in salted water. Drain and cool. Cut a lengthwise slice from each squash and scoop out the inside, to make a boat of the shell. Mix the meat with egg, seasonings, salt and pepper to taste, and brown in a heavy skillet. When the meat is brown, add the scooped-out insides of the squash and mix well. Spoon this mixture into boats. Place them in a shallow baking dish, well greased with butter or margarine. Spoon the Cheddar cheese soup over the top and bake in a preheated oven at 375 degrees for forty-five minutes.

Serve with creamed potatoes, a green vegetable and hot rolls, followed by a dessert of cake or pie.

This will serve four persons.

STEW OF DEER, ELK, MOOSE OR ANTELOPE

Any of the above meats may be used in this one-dish meal, with turnips and okra to give it zest.

4 pounds choice stew meat	1 No. 2 can stewed tomatoes
4 potatoes, cut in half	1 package frozen okra, or half
6 carrots, cut into two- or three-inch pieces	a pound of fresh if available
	1 large onion
4 turnips, left whole unless they are large	Salt
	Pepper
3 tablespoons bacon fat or cooking oil	Garlic salt
	Flour

Cut the meat into two-inch pieces and dust with salt, pepper, garlic salt and flour. Place three tablespoons of bacon fat or cooking oil in a heavy skillet or Dutch oven, and chop the onion into it. When lightly browned, add the meat and sear all the pieces over medium heat. When they are well seared, add hot water to cover and then the tomatoes, plus two tablespoons of Worcestershire sauce. Cover and leave simmering for one hour. Then add the potatoes, carrots, flour and turnips. Cook until the ingredients are almost tender, or approximately one hour. Cut the okra into two- or three-inches pieces and cook for about ten minutes, or until they are tender.

Serve with a romaine and green onion salad to which you have added your favorite oil dressing. We prefer cornbread muffins or cornbread sticks with stew. Jello makes a good light dessert to end this meal.

POT PIE WITH DEER, ELK OR MOOSE

Pot pie on a restaurant menu is always a quick sellout, but have you ever tried it with venison? This recipe, again, is a meal in itself.

2 pounds venison stew meat, cut into one-inch cubes	2 large potatoes, cut into two-inch pieces
1 teaspoon salt	6 carrots, sliced or cut into cubes
½ teaspoon pepper	
1 teaspoon Worcestershire sauce	½ green pepper
3 tablespoons bacon fat	2 packages canned biscuits (or make your own)
1 large onion, quartered	

Sauté the meat in bacon fat. Add salt and Worcestershire sauce. When the meat is well browned, pour in enough water to cover, add vegetables and cook for another thirty minutes. If necessary, add more water. Place the biscuits on top of the meat and vegetables and bake in a preheated oven at 375 degrees until the biscuits are well browned.

Serve with tossed green salad or fruit salad. Dessert might be pecan pie with whipped cream, if you're not a calorie-counter.

This will serve four hearty eaters.

RAGOUT OF MOOSE, ELK OR DEER

A ragout is nothing more than well-seasoned meat and vegetables cooked in a thick sauce. It is another way to use stew meat, yet it isn't exactly a stew. Try this appetizing dish on the family, and watch them go for seconds.

2 pounds stew meat cut into cubes	1 tablespoon Worcestershire sauce
3 tablespoons bacon fat	¼ teaspoon celery seed
1 small green onion, finely chopped	½ teaspoon parsley
	Salt
1 small green pepper, finely chopped	Pepper
	Flour

Sprinkle the meat with salt and pepper, and cover generously with flour. In a heavy skillet, brown the meat in bacon fat. Add onion, green pepper, celery seed and parsley, and when these are well heated add the Worcestershire sauce and just enough water to cover the meat. Cover the pan and simmer until meat is tender, or approximately one and a half hours. Check occasionally to make sure there is sufficient liquid to keep from burning. If the gravy is not thick enough, you may add a little flour paste to thicken.

Serve with buttered carrots and green salad, followed by gooseberry pie.

This recipe will serve four people.

POT ROAST OF MOOSE OR ELK

For this dish, choose either a seven-bone or a wedge-cut roast.

4 to 5 pounds moose or elk roast	Pepper
	Garlic powder
3 tablespoons bacon fat	Salt
2 large onions, quartered	Flour

Melt the bacon fat in a Dutch oven or heavy skillet with a tight-fitting lid. Wipe the meat dry with paper towels and sprinkle with salt, pepper and garlic powder. Dredge with flour and brown in bacon fat until all sides are seared and the flour is brown, being careful not to let it burn. Add onions and enough water to cover the bottom of the stew pan to a depth of about half an inch. Reduce the flame and simmer for one and a half hours. Replace water as necessary, and turn the roast to prevent burning and sticking.

Serve with macaroni and cheese, stewed tomatoes, and a tossed green salad, with sherbert or ice cream for dessert.

ELK RIBS AND DUMPLINGS

Here is another rib recipe to prove that game meat is just as versatile as beef. The ribs of either elk or moose are very good prepared this way.

3½ pounds ribs of elk or moose	1 teaspoon garlic powder
1 onion, sliced	Salt
1 No. 303 can stewed tomatoes	Pepper
3 tablespoons bacon fat	Water
1 tablespoon Worcestershire sauce	Rogers' dumplings (see recipe on page 141)

Salt, pepper and flour the ribs and brown in bacon grease. Add more flour if necessary to take up all the bacon fat. Add enough water to cover the meat; then add stewed tomatoes, garlic powder, onion and Worcestershire sauce. Cover and cook for two hours, or until the ribs are tender. Add the dumplings and cook until done, or for about fifteen or twenty minutes more.

We find a nice crisp salad is all that is needed with this dish, which will serve four.

ELK SWISS STEAK

Elk, moose or deer meat may be used in this recipe.

2 or 3 pounds round steak from elk or moose	½ teaspoon garlic powder
1 medium onion, sliced	3 or 4 tablespoons bacon fat
1 small green pepper, sliced	Salt
1 No. 303 can solid pack tomatoes	Pepper
	Flour

Salt, pepper and flour the meat, using a meat mallet to pound in as much flour as possible. Cut into serving pieces and brown in bacon fat in a large heavy skillet. Add garlic powder, tomatoes and sufficient water to cover the meat, and simmer for thirty minutes. Turn the meat, place rings of onion and pepper on top, and add enough water so the onion and pepper are covered. Cook until tender, or for thirty to forty-five minutes.

Serve with buttered baked potatoes, Brussels sprouts, hot biscuits and a green salad.

This will serve four to six persons.

VENISON IN BARBECUE SAUCE

This is a tasty way to use up a venison roast left over from a previous meal, and a dish the whole family will enjoy.

3 or 4 pounds leftover venison roast, boned and shredded or cut into serving pieces	3 tablespoons liquid smoke (more if desired)
1 bottle tomato catsup	1 can tomato sauce
1 medium-sized onion, cut fine	Salt
1 medium-sized clove garlic	Pepper

Place the meat in a baking dish. Mix remaining ingredients, pour over it and cook slowly for about an hour and a half. Serve piping hot, with potato chips or French-fries and warmed sandwich buns. Children especially like it this way.

VENISON SAUSAGE

Here is a good venison sausage recipe picked up from some friends in Arkansas.

12 pounds meat, half venison, half pork
1½ tablespoons rubbed sage
1 tablespoon garlic powder
¼ cup salt
1½ tablespoons black pepper
1 tablespoon saltpeter (sodium nitrate)
¼ teaspoon allspice
1 tablespoon crushed chili pepper (optional)

Cut venison and pork into small chunks for the grinder. Add all the seasonings, mix thoroughly, and put through the grinder, using a medium blade. Pack the meat in sausage bags or casings and hang it for long smoking at a low temperature. If you wish, the meat may be stored in a freezer and used as you would a good pork sausage. But smoking certainly adds much to the flavor, and is well worth the effort.

VENISON PEPPERONI

This is a good sausage that may be used in making pizza, as an hors d'oeuvre, or for nibbling with crackers and a cold beer.

5 pounds ground venison from elk, deer or antelope
2 pounds pork
1½ pounds beef suet
1 teaspoon ginger
½ teaspoon cardamon
1 teaspoon red pepper
¾ teaspoon ground white pepper
1 teaspoon crushed peppercorns
1 teaspoon garlic powder
1 teaspoon oregano
2 teaspoons fennel seed

Using a medium blade, grind the venison, pork and beef suet together. When the meat reaches room temperature, mix all the other ingredients into the meat, blending them in thoroughly. Let stand two or three hours. Stuff into sausage casings, and follow standard directions for smoking.

POLISH VENISON SAUSAGE

Polish sausage is an excellent way of using some of the trimmings left from processing venison. As for many other sausage mixes, everyone has his own method. This is the one we like. It makes an excellent breakfast sausage.

5 pounds ground lean venison
5 pounds ground lean pork
2 pounds beef suet
½ teaspoon coarse ground pepper

4 tablespoons salt (more if desired)
2 teaspoons crushed red chili peppers
2 tablespoons rubbed sage
1 teaspoon nutmeg

Grind the beef suet in with venison and pork (using a medium blade) and mix the rest of the ingredients into the meat. When you think you have it seasoned just right, fry a small sample on the stove and taste it. You may wish to add a little more of various seasonings to suit your own particular taste. Place in plastic bags (one-pound size for a family of two), and store in the freezer for future use. Since pork should not be kept frozen for over six months, try to use it up within that time. If a smoked sausage is desired, stuff the meat in sausage casings and smoke as you would any other sausage.

SMOKED SAUSAGE, ITALIAN STYLE

This smoked sausage may be used in making pizza, and is also an excellent hors d'oeuvre to serve to your guests. Warming it slightly enriches the flavor, bringing out the full strength of the spices.

5 pounds ground venison (deer, elk or antelope)	1 teaspoon thyme
1½ pounds beef suet	1 tablespoon crushed peppercorns
3 tablespoons salt	1 teaspoon ground pepper
2 tablespoons sugar	1 tablespoon chili powder
2 teaspoons ground cumin	2 tablespoons ground oregano

Using a medium blade, grind the venison with the beef suet. When the meat has reached room temperature, mix all the seasonings into the meat and let it stand for several hours so that the meat can absorb the flavor completely.

This sausage should be smoked; follow the usual instructions.

Serve with crisp crackers.

SMOKED VENISON SALAMI SAUSAGE

This isn't exactly a salami, but it is similar in taste and we find it delicious.

5 pounds ground venison (deer, elk or antelope)	½ teaspoon ground cloves
1½ pounds beef suet	2 teaspoons garlic powder
3 tablespoons salt	1½ teaspoon nutmeg
2 tablespoons sugar	1 teaspoon ground pepper
2 tablespoons cayenne pepper	2 teaspoons crushed peppercorns

Using a medium blade, grind the venison and beef suet together, and let the meat stand until it reaches room temperature. Mix all seasonings into the meat thoroughly, and let stand at room temperature for several hours to absorb the flavor completely. Stuff into sausage casings and smoke according to standard instructions.

PICKLED TONGUE OR HEART OF VENISON

This pickling method will provide you with a real delicacy, and we venture to say that once you have tried it you'll save the heart of your venison and the tongue of the elk and moose. The tongue of the deer may also be used, although it is smaller.

2 teaspoons whole cloves   1 onion
1 bay leaf   ½ teaspoon pepper
4 cups vinegar   ½ teaspoon mustard seed
1 tablespoon salt

Wash and clean the meat and boil until tender. For tongue, remove the skin.

Combine the remaining ingredients and boil for thirty minutes. Add two cups of the broth in which the meat was cooked, strain and pour over the meat. Let it stand in the refrigerator for three days before serving.

May be served as an hors d'oeuvre or as a snack with horseradish or mustard and rye bread.

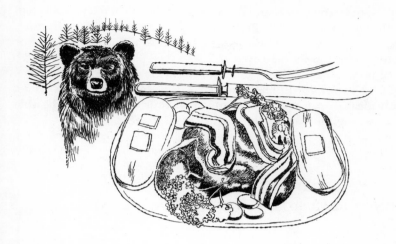

Black Bear

Although bears are usually thought of as flesh-eating animals, or carnivores, they also feed on berries, grubs, nuts, honey and the tender roots of various plants and shrubs. The black bear of North America is the best known and the most common species. Though it is considered less dangerous than the grizzly and some others, a black sow bear with young cubs can be a real menace if you molest her, or if you unknowingly come between her and the cubs.

This is the smallest of North American bears, some specimens weighing around five hundred pounds but the average around three hundred. The record black bear, killed in Arizona, weighed nine hundred pounds—an unusual specimen!

Despite their name, these bears are not always black. Some have patches of white on the face and chest, and some are solid brown or cinnamon-colored. Their life span is from fifteen to twenty years.

As a rule, bears are not hunted for food as one hunts deer, elk or other venison, though many are killed during the search for other game. Many hunters take home only the head and hide and have them tanned to make a bear rug for the den.

There is much controversy on whether or not bear meat is edible and, if so, as to its quality. Some people say that a bear killed shortly after coming out of hibernation in the spring, when it has lost all its surplus fat, or one that has been on a berry or grub diet for some time, is very good eating. Frankly, we are not fond of bear meat. However, the portion of the one we ate had been taken from a bear killed late in the fall, when it was ready to hibernate, and was extremely fat. While cooking, it didn't give off the rank odor that some say is present in cooking bear, and the meat was very tender; but it had a flavor we did not especially like. Perhaps if it had been marinated in fancy wines and sauces it would have been better, but in so doing the true flavor of the bear would have been destroyed.

A friend of mine cooked a large amount of bear by the deep-pit barbecue method and said it was good. The few recipes that follow are the ways we prepared bear meat. If you try them, or others of your own, you will be able to form your own opinion about the quality of bear meat.

BONED BEAR ROAST WITH BARBECUE SAUCE

We have found that this method of preparing bear meat improves its eating qualities considerably.

5 pounds bear roast, boned   Pepper
Salt

Wipe the roast with a damp cloth and be sure all the fat has been trimmed from the meat. Brush it with open pit barbecue sauce (see recipe on page 148) and let it stand for at least thirty minutes. Place the meat on aluminum foil, brush again with sauce and roast in a 325-degree oven for two and a half or three hours. Do not cover the roast, and baste it frequently. Bear, like pork, should always be well done.

Serve with mashed potatoes, a green vegetable and a salad of lettuce wedges with mayonnaise.

BEAR LEG ROAST

4 pounds bear leg   Thyme
Salt   Flour
Pepper   3 strips bacon

Be sure the roast is well cleaned, and that all the bear fat has been trimmed off. Generously sprinkle the meat with salt, pepper and thyme and dust with flour. Place on a rack in the roasting pan and lay the strips of bacon over it. Preheat the oven to 350 degrees and cook for two and a half to three hours. Bear meat, like pork, should be thoroughly cooked.

Serve on a platter garnished with baked yams, and accompany with Brussels sprouts and a tossed salad in an oil and vinegar dressing. For dessert, we suggest pumpkin pie.

BROILED BEAR LOIN CHOPS

2 chops per serving   Pepper
Salt

Be sure you have trimmed all the fat from the chops. Salt and pepper to taste, and place under the broiler in a pan covered with aluminum foil. Cook for eight to ten minutes, or until the chops are nicely browned. Turn and cook on the other side until brown, or for approximately eight minutes. The meat should now be well done; if it is not, cook a little longer.

Serve with French-fried or baked potatoes, a crisp tossed green salad with your favorite oil dressing, and buttered toast.

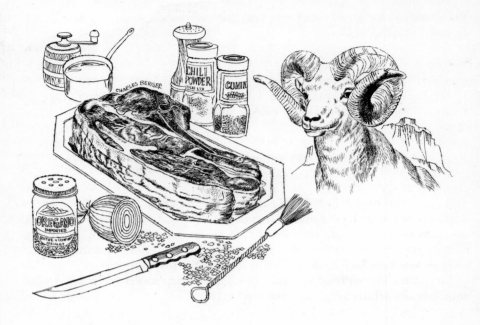

Rocky Mountain
Bighorn Sheep

The Rocky Mountain bighorn sheep is a symbol of the wilderness in the Western part of the United States and Canada. Once near extinction, this beautiful animal has been saved through a carefully planned conservation program, and the outlook for its future is now very promising. Special recognition must be given to the Montana and Idaho Game Departments for their ceaseless efforts to thwart extinction of the animal. Other Rocky Mountain States also have contributed their share to the program. By issuing only special hunting permits in selected areas, the game departments have controlled the yearly harvest and kept the herds in balance.

In the 1920's the entire sheep population of the United States was estimated to be about 28,000; figures released by the Fish and Wildlife Service in 1952 showed it had declined to slightly more than 17,000 head. This abrupt decline was not the result of hunting pressure alone, for quite often entire herds in remote and almost inaccessible areas were wiped out or severely decimated.

The major decline of the bighorn occurred between 1870 and 1880, when scores of sheep died of what now appears to have been scabies. This and other diseases of epidemic proportions took a tremendous toll of the sheep herds. Lung disease, similar to shipping fever of domestic animals, also has been one of the chief killers.

Much available evidence indicates that Rocky Mountain bighorn herds once roamed the prairie and valleys many miles from the nearest mountains, but encroachment of civilization and competition for food forced them to flee to the more rugged terrain where they are found today. Though the food is scarce and the winters more severe, they seem to prefer this type of terrain. In the summer, their range is usually at 8,000 feet or more above sea level. Their diet consists almost exclusively of low-growing herbage. A light snowfall will force them to lower, snow-free pastures.

In their daily life, mountain sheep do not follow any special routine, and their pattern of behavior is unpredictable. Contrary to some beliefs, old rams and ewes do not act as sentinels to sound an alarm in case of danger. They are reported to be the most easily approached game species in Idaho, and quite often you can walk within fifty feet of them when they are on a winter range.

One of the peculiarities of the bighorn is that it will become alarmed more easily when it sights you at a distance than at close range. It has been found that the best way to approach a herd is to appear in plain sight *below them,* approach very slowly, but in a *quartering direction,* remaining in sight at all times. By using this method it has been possible to walk within fifty feet of them. However, if you approach from above, they will quickly stampede at the first sight of you.

Curiosity or indifference are more frequent reactions to human beings than is fear. Like the antelope, mountain sheep are attracted by a strange or unknown object, and if you remain perfectly still they will sometimes approach within a very few feet of you.

They prefer to travel in bands with as many as twelve rams in one band. However, the mature ram will not run with ewes until the rutting season, so if you are hunting early in the season and sight a band of ewes, move to another area for there will be no legal rams in the immediate vicinity. Mountain sheep are quite sociable and often have been seen grazing with a herd of mule deer, even frolicking with them; but a frightened deer will cause a band of sheep to stampede, though the hunter is far away.

A mature bighorn sheep, field dressed, will weigh 175 to 200 pounds. Many who have eaten the meat claim that it is far superior to any other game animal. The Rocky Mountain bighorn surpasses the desert bighorn in this respect because of the abundance of good food and water in its habitat.

While the services of a guide aren't *absolutely* necessary, they are recommended when hunting the Rocky Mountain species because of the rugged terrain, the dangers of abrupt weather changes, and the special equipment needed for trips into mountainous areas. Also, unless you are thoroughly familiar with the range and habits of this animal, you might spend days in the woods and not even find any spoor, let alone a legal ram.

Arizona Desert Bighorn Sheep

The Arizona bighorn sheep is considered one of the Big Ten among game animals, and is one of the most highly prized. It was not transplanted to Arizona as elk was, but is a longtime resident. The last big glacial retreat is said to have occurred over twelve thousand years ago, and it is possible that the bighorn became established in this area at that time.

From the start, it has had a bitter battle for survival, in a habitat of desert wastes, barren mountain peaks and sparse vegetation, causing the sheep to range long distances in their search for food. The average rainfall in the area is approximately three and a half inches per year, and the temperatures vary from just below freezing, on the winter nights, to above 125 degrees in summer, when quite often the ground temperatures on the black rock formation may exceed 150 degrees.

The first white settlers who came to Arizona reported bighorn in abundance. Hundreds of prospectors for gold and other minerals slaughtered them for food; trophy hunters killed them for their heads, leaving behind the carcass to decay; and the sheep contracted diseases from domestic stock that roamed the desert, where competition for the limited amount of food and water was keen. Under such adverse conditions, it is no wonder that their numbers were reduced to a pitiful few.

For over fifty years there was no open season on these animals, and their slowly decreasing numbers made it appear that they would soon become extinct. In 1937 nearly one and a half million acres were set aside for them in an arid, desolate region now known as the Cabeza Prieta and Kofa game ranges. Natural water tanks were enlarged, and retention dams were built in an attempt to provide the sheep with a constant water supply. In an extensive program to eliminate competition, the numbers of predators, burros and other feral animals were reduced, and patrols were increased to stamp out poaching. Under this closely supervised program, the numbers of the sheep slowly increased. But it is easy to see that the desert bighorn had to be a sturdy animal to survive at all under such adverse conditions. In 1950 its numbers were estimated to be almost eleven hundred head, about forty-five per cent of these along the Colorado River.

The first Arizona bighorn hunt in many years was held in January 1953, on a limited-permit drawing basis—a procedure that is still being followed.

The bighorn is not a large animal, but rams of legal size will usually average around 150 pounds undressed, sometimes more but quite often less. Owing to the scarcity of food and water, the Arizona bighorn is not as large on the average as its cousin the Rocky Mountain bighorn, whose supply of food and water is plentiful, and which lives in a climate more suitable for a grazing animal. It is the opinion of all guides in the north woods country, and of hunters who have consumed the meat, that the Rocky Mountain bighorn is unsurpassed for flavor and texture.

The desert bighorn is also delicious, but it must be properly handled owing to the extreme heat of its habitat even in midwinter. It should be skinned as quickly as possible, and hung so that air can circulate around it freely, dissipating the body heat. The carcass must be covered with a porous cloth to protect it from flies and other insects.

Unless you are thoroughly familiar with the range and feeding habits of this wary animal, for hunting it is advisable to hire a competent guide, who as a rule can also provide you with the special equipment needed. The most acute sense of the bighorn sheep is its sight, upon which it relies, like the pronghorn antelope, to warn it of approaching danger.

To get a real trophy is usually the result of endless climbing and stalking, climbing and stalking. But a kill, once you have made it, will be the climax of one of your most thrilling hunts, and the trophy will be one you can point to with genuine pride.

ROAST BIGHORN SHEEP

This recipe was given to me by Mr. Bob Householder, senior Arizona desert bighorn sheep guide, who at the time had seventeen guided kills to his credit. He is also well known for his articles in widely circulated outdoor magazines. He told me he had given this recipe to nearly three hundred Arizona sheep hunters who had made kills in the past fourteen years.

4 or 5 pounds sheep roast from the leg or loin
1 cup cooking vinegar
1 tablespoon Adolph's meat tenderizer
1 package dry onion soup
1 cup red port wine
2 tablespoons cayenne pepper (optional)
Salt
Pepper

Mix the vinegar with an equal amount of water, add tenderizer and pour into a roasting pan. Brush the mixture thoroughly over the roast, cover and let it stand for approximately two hours. Drain off the liquid, salt and pepper to taste (adding cayenne pepper if desired), and pour in the wine and the dry onion soup. Place a tight-fitting lid on the roaster and bake in a moderate oven for approximately two hours, or until the roast is tender. Check frequently to make sure the liquid does not evaporate. If it becomes low, add a little water and baste the roast with the residue from the bottom of the pan. When done, serve on a large platter garnished with sliced oranges and green parsley.

Slice the meat as you serve it with mashed potatoes, string beans, warm hard rolls or French bread, and a salad of lettuce wedges with mayonnaise or your favorite dressing. For dessert, serve sherbet or ice cream.

ROAST LOIN OF BIGHORN SHEEP

Any sportsman who has eaten properly cared-for sheep will tell you that it tops everything for tastiness among large game animals. This is doubly true of the Rocky Mountain bighorn sheep. A chuck roast from the blade will do in the event that you have cut the loin into chops.

3 or 4 pounds bighorn roast, from the loin or chuck
1 clove garlic
Salt
Pepper
Flour

Wipe the roast with a damp cloth. Cut two or three gashes in the meat and insert slivers of garlic. Salt and pepper, sprinkle with flour and place uncovered in a 375- to 400-degree oven for thirty minutes to sear or brown lightly. Reduce heat to moderate (325 degrees), and roast for about two and a half hours, longer if necessary to make it tender. Gravy may be made from some of residue in the roaster.

Serve with mint jelly, potatoes, a green vegetable, and a salad of lettuce wedges and your favorite dressing.

OVEN- OR CHARCOAL-BROILED CHOPS OF BIGHORN SHEEP

The chops of the bighorn sheep should be at least one inch thick. You will find them as succulent as any lamb chops you've ever eaten.

2 chops per person   Salt
  (more for big eaters)   Pepper
Butter or margarine

Melt the butter or margarine, brush the top side of the chops and place under the broiler or on a grill over charcoal. Under the broiler, cook for about eight minutes; over charcoal—and not too close to the fire—cook about ten minutes. Turn and butter the other side and cook about five minutes more under the broiler, or ten more over charcoal. The meat should then be medium well done. Cook longer if desired, but to do so will destroy some of the delicate and distinctive flavor of the chops. Salt and pepper after removing from the fire.

Serve with French-fried potatoes, buttered toast and asparagus vinaigrette with hard-boiled egg as a salad.

BLADE OR CHUCK ROAST OF BIGHORN SHEEP

This is the favorite way of preparing a bighorn sheep roast along the Mexican border, as the flavorings suggest.

3 pounds blade roast of
bighorn sheep
1 tablespoon chili sauce with
equal parts of water
1 medium-sized onion,
chopped fine
¼ cup cooking oil or olive oil

1 teaspoon chili powder
½ teaspoon cumin
½ teaspoon oregano
1 teaspoon salt
1 teaspoon coarsely ground
pepper

Wipe the roast with a dry cloth, and brush with oil. Mix the dry seasonings in a bowl and rub thoroughly into all sides of roast. Place meat in a heavy roaster with a rack in the bottom. Mix all seasonings, including the oil, in a cup of water and pour into the roaster. Finish filling with water to the bottom of the rack, but do not let the water touch the meat. Roast in a 400-degree oven for thirty minutes, reduce to 325 degrees and continue roasting until meat is tender and done. Add additional water if necessary, and baste frequently with drippings in the bottom of the roaster.

A blade roast cooked this way will stimulate the taste buds of the most critical. Brought in on a large platter garnished with baked oranges and parsley, it is truly a regal dish.

With it, serve creamed potatoes, a green vegetable, and asparagus vinaigrette with hard-boiled eggs. A light red wine will be excellent with this meal. For dessert, if you still have room, serve jello.

SHANK OF BIGHORN SHEEP

You will find the shank of the bighorn sheep as tasty as that of the domestic breed, and we like it cooked this way rather than cut up for burgers or stew. The flavor is excellent, and the meat, properly prepared, will be tender and juicy, practically falling off the bone.

We use the same recipe for this as we do for preparing the shank of antelope or deer. See the recipe for venison shank à la Montana, on page 14. Allow one shank per serving. We use only the front shank unless the animal is below average in size.

BIGHORN SHEEP STEW

2 pounds choice bighorn stew meat, cut into bite size

1 can lima beans

1 can string beans or peas

1 medium-sized onion, quartered

2 medium-sized potatoes, peeled and quartered

4 carrots cut into one-inch pieces

1 green pepper, chopped (optional)

¾ teaspoon salt

½ teaspoon pepper

1 tablespoon bacon fat or cooking oil

In a large, heavy kettle or Dutch oven, brown the stew meat in bacon fat over a fairly hot fire. Remove from the fire and add potatoes, onion, carrots, salt and pepper. Cover with water and simmer forty-five minutes. Add lima and string beans or peas during the last fifteen minutes of cooking. If desired, a small amount of flour paste may be added to thicken the stew. If you use green pepper, add it at same time you do the potatoes, carrots and onion.

Serve with a tossed salad and sourdough French bread.

BIGHORN SHEEP PATTIES

If you're fond of lamb patties, you will like these equally well.

1 pound ground sheep meat

1 tablespoon canned milk

¼ teaspoon oregano

6 strips bacon

Salt

Pepper

Mix the meat thoroughly with milk and oregano, and sprinkle with salt and pepper. From the one pound of meat you should get four to six patties about four inches in diameter, the number depending upon how thick you want them. Wrap each patty in a strip of bacon, fasten with a toothpick and place in a broiler pan which has been covered with aluminum foil. Cook about eight to ten minutes on each side, depending upon how well done you like your meat.

Serve with creamed potatoes, string beans or peas, and a tossed green salad.

This will serve two hearty eaters.

Collared Peccary or Javelina

The collared peccary, which in the Southwest is commonly called the javelina (pronounced *havelina*), is a relative of the wild hog, but quite unlike it. Javelinas are found in parts of Texas and New Mexico, and in the southern deserts of Arizona. They stand less than two feet high at the shoulder, and average around thirty-five or forty pounds when field dressed. The javelina is one of the smallest animals to be hunted as a trophy.

In Arizona, since the game department has learned that the javelina doesn't have any special breeding season as deer, antelope and other game do, but breeds the year round, spring hunts are permitted. Hunting javelina can be a most pleasant experience, since as a rule the weather will be mild. You will soon discover that the animal is well camouflaged, blending in with the sparse vegetation and shadows, so that to secure one is a real challenge. For so small an animal a large-caliber rifle isn't necessary, but experts do recommend using a rifle with a flat trajectory, since you will be lucky if you get a standing shot, and may have to aim from a distance.

Javelinas are hardy but very timid, and will usually flee at the slightest sign of danger. They always run downhill, never up, and always with their long canine teeth clattering and gnashing—so that a hunter who meets them will think he is being attacked by a herd of vicious, man-eating pigs when in reality they are only trying to get past him.

The javelina's tough, pliable skin, when tanned, can be made into the finest of gloves and jackets. As to the edibility of the meat there are two schools of thought. Some say the animal is fit only for a trophy. Others say that barbecued javelina is excellent, and in the Southwest each year many are eaten that way.

In dressing a javelina, extreme caution must be used not to cut or rupture the musk gland, which is located in the center and toward the rear of the back. The slightest amount of this musk on the meat, or even on the knife blade if you continue to use it without washing, will make it unfit to eat.

BARBECUED JAVELINA

This is another recipe given to me by Bob Householder, the noted Arizona guide and outdoor writer, who as of 1966 had guided a total of 201 javelina kills from his camp.

5 or 6 pounds javelina meat, cleaned and boned	2 teaspoons cayenne pepper
	½ cup cooking oil
1 pint red port wine	Salt
1 pint cider vinegar	Pepper

Be sure the animal has been skinned immediately after the kill, that it has been hung in the shade to cool completely, and that it has been protected from the flies which are so prevalent in the spring on the deserts of the Southwest. Have the meat boned out, and if any fat is present remove it. Mix oil, wine, vinegar, salt, pepper and cayenne and marinate the meat in this mixture for about three hours. Remove; and again sprinkle with salt, black pepper and cayenne. Place in a lightly oiled roaster and bake in a moderate oven until the meat is done. Baste frequently with the marinade.

BRINE-CURED JAVELINA

Here is a way of preparing javelina that does away with the strong, musky odor that accompanies meat of this sort unless it is properly prepared. Many people cook it in a deep-pit barbecue, but this usually necessitates cooking the whole animal. Using the brine curing method will enable you to cook only what you need for each meal, eliminating needless waste.

First be sure the animal has been carefully skinned and cooled, and that the musk gland on its back has not been cut or ruptured. Remove the front and hind legs and take out the bones, leaving the meat in chunks as large as possible. Cut the ribs from the backbone, as near to the loin as you can; then cut chops to the desired thickness, stacking them in the order they were cut, and removing any fat that may be present.

With the point of a knife, pierce the large chunks in one or two places and push a whole clove into each cut. Place the boned meat and the chops in a large crock, a glass jar or a wooden keg. Mix enough Morton's Tender-Quick to cover the meat completely. If it shows a tendency to come to the top, weight it down with a crock or porcelain dish, so that the meat will remain submerged at all times.

After about fifteen days, depending upon the temperature, the meat should be cured. Upon being removed from the jar it will have a dull, unappetizing look, but don't let that worry you. Drain the meat and place in plastic bags in family-sized lots. Once the meat is cooked, it will take on a deep, rich red color.

BOILED JAVELINA DINNER

This method of cooking brine-cured javelina is very similar to a New England boiled dinner using venison.

2 pounds cured javelina meat	8 carrots, cut in half (two per serving)
8 medium-sized potatoes, peeled but left whole (allow at least two potatoes per serving)	1 average-sized head cabbage
	3 or 4 strips beef suet, one-half inch thick

Place the meat in a large stew pot, cover with cold water and bring to a boil. Pour this water off—a step necessary to de-salt the cured meat. If necessary, slit the meat in such a manner that you can secure the beef suet with butchers' twine; or it may be pinned on with toothpicks. Rub thoroughly with coarsely ground pepper, replace in the stew pot, cover with water and simmer for two and a half or three hours, or until the meat is tender. Remove the meat, place potatoes and carrots in the broth, and cook until almost done. Cut the cabbage into wedges, add to the broth and cook for six to eight minutes, or until the cabbage is done but still firm. Do not overcook it. Arrange the vegetables on a platter and cover with thinly sliced, deep red javelina meat. Serve with crisp corn bread sticks. For four to six persons.

Cottontail Rabbit

The cottontail rabbit provides sport for more people than any game animal in the United States. Each year, over 50,000,000 rabbits are taken; figured at an average of one and a half pounds apiece, this adds up to the staggering sum of 75,000,000 pounds of meat! To withstand such hunting pressure, an animal has to be highly prolific, and of course the rabbit has a reputation for being just that.

As a youngster I spent many happy hours in the woods with my old hound Red, hunting this little animal. At an age when I was still not allowed to own a gun, I would wait until old Red treed the rabbit and then, using a long, slender hickory limb with a fork at the end, I would twist the rabbit out of the hollow. If I could not reach it that way, I would build a fire and then smother the blaze with green or wet leaves so as to send up a column of choking smoke. As the rabbit backed out I would grab it—or if I missed, the chase would be on again. In wet woods where I was unable to start a wood fire, I would sometimes pull off a long, ribbed black stocking and use it to smoke the rabbit out. Burning cloth was more effective than leaves, but of course I had to account for the missing stocking when I got home.

In those days we never heard of tularemia, an infectious disease of the cottontail that is dangerous if it enters the human blood stream. For this reason, cleanliness and caution should be exercised in handling rabbits. The chances of contracting the disease will be practically eliminated if you follow these simple rules:

1. Shoot only rabbits that are spry and active.
2. Don't hunt them except when the weather has been cool for several weeks.
3. Avoid cutting yourself or breaking the skin on your hands while cleaning them. Should you have an open wound, wear rubber gloves.
4. If you find the liver spotted, throw the rabbit away. The chances are that it has tularemia.
5. After cleaning, *wash your hands thoroughly,* being careful not to leave any dried blood under or around the fingernails. I always clean my hands with alcohol or some good disinfectant.
6. Cook the meat thoroughly.

Don't let all this deter you from the sport of hunting the cottontail, or from eating the meat. The disease isn't as prevalent as many suppose; and usually, where you find one rabbit with it, others in the same area will have it also, and in a short time all will be wiped out. If you see a rabbit running "to beat sixty," you can almost be certain it is healthy.

I have never personally known anyone who had been infected with the disease. But that doesn't mean it is nonexistent, and the precautions should always be observed in handling rabbits.

FRIED RABBIT

A young cottontail, properly prepared, is as delectable as a small game dish can be. Among the numerous ways of cooking it, my favorite is frying. One rabbit will serve two persons.

1 rabbit, cleaned, for each two persons	Pepper
	Cooking oil
Salt	Flour

Cut the rabbit into pieces for frying as you would a chicken. Salt and pepper and thoroughly dredge in flour. Place in a heavy skillet, to which you have added cooking oil to a depth of approximately one-fourth inch, heated medium hot. Brown slowly on one side then turn and brown the other side. If the rabbit is old and inclined to be tough, cover and let it simmer a few minutes until tender.

When the meat is tender, remove it, dissolve a tablespoon of flour in a cup of water, and pour into the skillet to make gravy. Stir constantly, adding milk or flour until the desired thickness is reached.

Serve with fluffy steamed rice, hot biscuits and a green salad or vegetable, followed by a dessert of pie or ice cream.

OVEN-FRIED RABBIT

We first used this recipe for cooking domestic rabbit, but find that it works just as well for a young, tender wild rabbit.

2 young rabbits, cleaned and cut up	¾ cup flour
¼ cup butter or margarine	1 tablespoon salt
¼ cup cooking oil	½ teaspoon pepper

Cut off the front and hind legs of the rabbit, and divide the hind legs into two pieces, cutting at the joint. Cut the back into about four pieces, splitting it at the saddle. Mix the flour, salt and pepper and dredge each piece in the mixture. Place the floured pieces in a well-oiled shallow pan. Melt the butter, mix with the cooking oil, and pour over the rabbit, which should be only one layer deep in the pan. Bake in a 375-degree oven for one and a half hours. After the first forty-five minutes turn each piece to brown on the other side. If the rabbits were very young, by the time the meat is golden brown it should be just about ready to fall off the bone.

Serve with fluffy buttered rice, green peas and hot biscuits.

RABBIT AND ROGERS' DUMPLINGS

2 rabbits, cleaned and cut up to frying size	Pepper
¼ teaspoon thyme	Flour
2 bay leaves	1 teaspoon dried parsley
Salt	Cooking oil

Salt and pepper the rabbit; dredge in flour. Place in a heated heavy skillet to which you have added cooking oil, and sear on both sides.

Place the seared meat in a stew pot, cover with hot water, and add bay leaves, thyme and parsley. Place over a medium fire and cook until tender.

Make Rogers' dumplings, (see page 141), add to the stew pot and cook until done.

Serve with mashed potatoes, broccoli, hot rolls and fruit salad.

This will serve four people.

SMOTHERED RABBIT WITH ONIONS

Onion can be used as a seasoning with just about any meat dish you may prepare, and rabbit cooked this way is not disappointing. If you wish, a few slices of crisp bacon may be served on the side.

2 rabbits	4 strips bacon
1 large onion, sliced thin	(optional)
1 tablespoon Worcestershire	2 tablespoons bacon fat
sauce	Flour

Cut rabbit into pieces of frying size and sauté over a medium fire in a heavy skillet to which you have added a small amount of bacon fat. Salt and pepper. When the meat is brown, cover with thinly sliced onion and simmer approximately one hour under a loose-fitting cover. During the last few minutes of the simmering process, add a little water to the skillet; then, after removing the meat to a platter, add flour to make a medium thick gravy.

Serve with hot biscuits, string beans and mashed potatoes, followed by apple cobbler with cream for dessert.

This recipe serves two.

RABBIT AND DUMPLINGS

2 rabbits cut into pieces of	Salt
frying size	Pepper
¼ teaspoon thyme	Flour
2 bay leaves	1 teaspoon dried parsley
Cooking oil	

Salt and pepper rabbit to taste; dredge in flour. Place in a heavy skillet to which you have added a little cooking oil, and sear all the pieces on both sides. When thoroughly seared, place in a stew pot and cover with hot water. Add bay leaves, thyme and dried parsley. Cook over a medium fire until tender.

Make Rogers' dumplings (page 141), add to the stew pot and cook until done.

Serve with broccoli, mashed potatoes, hot rolls and a fruit salad. For four hearty eaters.

RABBIT POT PIE WITH VEGETABLES

A good meat pie is always welcome, and when made with a young, tender rabbit it is delicious. This recipe is a complete meal within itself.

2 medium-sized rabbits, cleaned and cut into pieces or quartered	1 small can peas or string beans
1 medium-sized onion, finely chopped	4 medium-sized carrots
2 medium-sized potatoes	1 tablespoon Worcestershire sauce
½ stick butter or margarine	Salt
	Pepper
	Flour

Place the rabbit in a stew pot, salt it and barely cover with water. Wash the potatoes and carrots thoroughly and add to the pot. Cover and cook over a medium fire about one hour.

When the meat is tender, remove, let it cool, and with your fingers remove all the meat from the bones. Melt the butter or margarine in a heavy skillet over a medium fire. Add the meat, the chopped onion, and the potatoes, peeled and diced, with salt and pepper to taste. Cook for five minutes, stirring constantly. When well seasoned and mixed, place the contents in the stew pot.

Measure the stock in which you have boiled the rabbit, and into each cupful stir one and a half tablespoons of flour. Cut the carrots into one-inch pieces; add them with the beans or peas and the Worcestershire sauce, and continue adding flour and water until the contents are covered. Make a thick pastry to cover the contents, place in a preheated oven at 350–375 degrees and bake until the crust is golden brown. If you prefer, you may use biscuits on top instead of the pastry crust.

Serve with a tossed salad and a light dessert.

The recipe will feed four or five persons.

Squirrel

Squirrels are among the most widely hunted of our small game animals. Of several American species, the fox squirrel of the Midwest, and ranging down into some of the Southern states, is the largest. It averages around two pounds, and occasionally one will weigh three pounds. Its coat is most often a reddish brown, though occasionally one will be almost black, and it is sometimes erroneously called the red squirrel, a name that correctly applies only to its much smaller Eastern cousin. The fox squirrel and the Eastern gray squirrel, which ranges from Minnesota to New England, and also through a portion of the South, are the two most widely hunted species.

Like much of our game, squirrels were valuable to the pioneers as a source of food, as well as of fur. Each year well over twenty-five million pounds of this delicate meat appear on the tables of American households.

There are several ways of hunting this wary little animal. Some use a small dog to tree the squirrel; some use the sneak method, and others the still hunt method. Though many use a shotgun, the most sporting way to take squirrels is with a 22-caliber rifle, making a good clean kill and at the same time improving your marksmanship.

74

As you walk slowly and quietly through the woods, a squirrel may make its presence known by dropping a nut, a pinecone or some other morsel of food as it goes about gathering and storing food for the winter. More often than not, it will be revealed by the flashing of its large bushy tail, or by the staccato bark as it scolds you or possibly a bluejay that has infringed upon its territory.

Many times if you are extremely quiet in a productive area, you can kill several squirrels with very little walking. Just to remain as quietly observant as possible takes patience and stealth. At times you may be confronted with a perplexing problem, and wish you could be on several sides of a tree at once; but any seasoned squirrel-hunter will have tricks up his sleeve to make the squirrel show itself.

It is best to hunt, of course, during the time the squirrels are most active. Like most game they can be found at nearly any hour of the day, but it is best to spend the midday or high noon period skinning and taking care of those you have killed in the early morning hours.

The meat of this little animal is less gamy in flavor than most other wild meat, and is a light red or almost pink in color. A young squirrel is a really tender, juicy, delicious piece of meat, worthy to grace the table of any gourmand.

FRIED YOUNG SQUIRREL

Squirrel meat, like that of any other animal, becomes tougher with age. This recipe is for the youngest and tenderest ones.

1 squirrel per person	Salt
Shortening	Pepper
Flour	

Clean the squirrel and cut it into pieces for frying. Rub with salt and pepper, dredge in flour and place the pieces one layer deep in a heavy skillet, in which you have placed shortening approximately one-fourth inch deep. Cook slowly over a medium fire until the meat is brown, then turn and brown the other side and remove from the skillet. To make gravy, place a heaping tablespoon of flour in the residue in the skillet and stir until it browns. Add milk and cook until the desired thickness is reached, then salt and pepper to taste.

Serve with fluffy steamed white rice, a green vegetable and hot biscuits. For dessert, serve sherbet or ice cream.

SQUIRREL STEW WITH DUMPLINGS

Here is an excellent way to cook a squirrel that is old and on the tough side.

1 squirrel per person, cut into pieces	Butter
Salt	Milk
Pepper	Dumplings

Salt and pepper the squirrel and place in a stew pot. Cover with water and bring to a boil. Keep the water at a slow boil until the meat is tender.

Make Rogers' dumplings (see recipe on page 141). Just before adding the dumplings, place approximately one-eighth pound of butter in the boiling water as seasoning. If the water is low, add milk to make a stock for cooking the dumplings. Continue to cook until the dumplings are done, or for approximately twelve or fifteen minutes.

Serve with buttered asparagus tips and sliced tomatoes. For dessert, we suggest apple pie with milk or cream.

BRUNSWICK STEW

Any squirrel hunter, or his wife, will have definite ideas of how a Brunswick stew should be made. We are no exception.

2 squirrels, cleaned and cut into several pieces	½ green pepper, chopped
1 can whole-kernel corn	1 package frozen okra (or half a pound of fresh if available)
1 can baby lima beans (frozen ones may be used)	1½ teaspoon salt
2 potatoes, quartered	¾ teaspoon pepper
1 onion, quartered	¼ pound butter (margarine may be used)

Salt and pepper the squirrels and place in a stew pot with enough water to cover completely (about one-half gallon). Cover and simmer for approximately one hour. Add potatoes, green pepper, onion, and okra and boil for about forty-five minutes more. Add lima beans, corn and butter, and cook fifteen minutes. If frozen limas are used, add to the stew along with the potatoes. If the vegetables are still not tender, cook a little longer. Tomatoes may be substituted for the okra.

TOUGH SQUIRREL, SMOTHERED

If a squirrel is very old—and any seasoned squirrel hunter will know whether it is—the chances are that it may be so tough as to require special handling. This method will make it tender and palatable.

1 squirrel per person	Salt
Shortening	Pepper
Flour	

Place the squirrel, either whole or cut into frying-size pieces, in lightly salted water and boil until tender. Remove and cool. Pepper and dredge in flour, and place the pieces one layer deep in a heavy skillet containing approximately a quarter inch of melted shortening. Cover and cook slowly over a medium fire browning on both sides. To make gravy, dissolve a heaping tablespoon of flour in a cup of the liquid in which you have boiled the squirrel. Pour this into the skillet with the residue. Add additional broth as needed, stirring constantly until the desired thickness has been reached. Salt and pepper to taste.

Serve with rice or mashed potatoes, a green vegetable, and piping hot biscuits, followed by your choice of pie for dessert.

Raccoon

The 'coon is an elusive nocturnal animal, and as a youngster I spent many nights chasing through the swamps with a pack of hounds until one was treed. At that time the Stutz Bear Cat and coonskin coat were the rage on college campuses, and a good prime coonskin would bring a price of six or eight dollars.

Raccoons are very intelligent, and can confuse a pack of hound dogs in a way that would put a fox to shame. It almost seems as though the 'coon enjoys the chase as much as the dogs, for it cooperates to the fullest extent by circling trees, walking rail fences, crossing streams a dozen times over and often swimming downstream to break the trail.

An old boar 'coon can hold his own with an inexperienced dog. More than once I've seen a dog tangle with a 'coon after being chased into a stream, and I have thought the dog would drown before he could break loose and swim to shore. I've also seen a dog refuse to accept the challenge of an old 'coon sitting on a stump or a partially submerged log.

You have no doubt often heard that a 'coon washes everything it eats. This isn't so, but its eating habits are clean, and its diet includes a variety of things such as corn, fruit, tender roots, eggs, birds, frogs, fish and so on. More than once I have lost a nice mess of bass to a pack of 'coons that had found them dangling in the water, tied to the boat or dock.

A baby 'coon can make a very interesting and comical pet, getting into more mischief than a monkey and providing many laughs. But as it reaches the adult stage it may become vicious, and inflict painful and serious bodily harm. Like all wild animals, raccoons can be trained but not tamed, and are not to be trusted very far.

The meat of the raccoon is dark and very fat, and the flavor and odor of the fat are so strong that it must all be removed before cooking. Also, as with squirrels and some other animals, you must watch out for the nodules or "kernels" under the front legs and the fleshy part of the hind legs. Since they are mostly covered with fat, by removing that you will get the "kernels" as well. They are each about the size of a bean, oblong and brown, and easy to identify.

As youngsters we hunted 'coons mostly for their fur and ate them only occasionally. What I am passing on to you here are a few ways they were prepared in our house. Perhaps you will know of a better way, but at the time I thought these were pretty good.

BAKED RACCOON

This is a good recipe for an older 'coon that may be on the tough side. If it is old, it will have badly worn teeth, possibly some of them broken, and perhaps a misshapen mouth. A middle-aged 'coon will have a full-set of teeth, which will be sharp and not worn. Either one should be parboiled to insure tenderness.

1 or 2 raccoons, cleaned	Salt
2 strips salt pork for each animal	Pepper
	2 bay leaves
1 apple for each animal	

Trim off all the fat and remove the kernels from each animal. Place in a roasting pan, fill about half full of water, cover and parboil about thirty minutes. Remove, and save the broth.

Rub salt and pepper on the animals, using more pepper than usual. Cut the apples in half and place one inside each animal. Pin the salt pork on the outside with toothpicks in such a manner that the fats will flow over the meat. Place in a 325-degree oven and baste occasionally with some of the broth and pork fats which have been added to the roaster. The meat should be brown and tender in about an hour and a half.

Serve with scalloped potatoes and green beans.

Two raccoons will feed four persons.

FRICASSEE OF YOUNG RACCOON

A fricassee is simply meat cooked in its own juices and gravy, and is always juicy and tender. A young 'coon prepared this way is no exception.

1 or 2 young raccoons, dressed	Flour
Salt	1 large onion, sliced
Pepper	Cooking oil

Be sure to remove the nodules or "kernels" under each leg, along with all the fat.

Cut the young 'coon into pieces of frying size. Salt and pepper them, dredge them in flour and sauté in a heavy skillet over fairly high heat. When browned on all sides, stir a heaping tablespoon of flour into a glass of water and pour it into the skillet, adding more water until the meat is almost covered. Add the sliced onion, cover and simmer about one hour. The meat will be tender and juicy and you will have an ample amount of gravy.

Serve with mashed potatoes, a green vegetable and piping hot biscuits. This will feed four hearty eaters.

ROAST RACCOON WITH DRESSING

1 or 2 dressed raccoons	1 teaspoon pepper
1 cup wine vinegar	½ teaspoon sweet basil
1 tablespoon salt	4 strips salt pork, sliced thin

Remove the fat and the kernels from the raccoons and place them whole on a rack in a large roasting pan. Add vinegar, salt and sweet basil, fill almost half full of water, cover and parboil for about thirty to forty-five minutes. This will tenderize the toughest old 'coon. Meanwhile, make this dressing:

1 package prepared poultry dressing, or make your own if you prefer	1 cup diced onions
	1 cup diced celery stalks
	¼ cup butter

Sauté the onion and celery in butter until tender and add to the dressing, mixing thoroughly. Stuff the raccoons as you would poultry. Skewer by inserting toothpicks through the flesh at the vent, and tie with butchers' twine.

Place salt pork on the outside in such a manner that the fat will flow over the meat. Bake in a moderate oven (325 degrees) until golden brown and tender.

Serve with mashed potatoes and a green vegetable. This should feed four to six persons.

ROAST OPOSSUM WITH DRESSING

The opossum is a very fat animal with a rich but tasty meat whose flavor is unlike that of any other game. Dress it much as you would a suckling pig, removing the entrails and also the head and tail if you wish.

1 opossum	½ teaspoon Worcestershire
1 tablespoon butter	sauce
1 large onion, chopped fine	1 hard-boiled egg, chopped fine
1 cup bread crumbs	Salt
¼ teaspoon crushed red	Pepper
pepper	6 sweet potatoes or yams

After it has been cleaned, wash the opossum inside and out with hot water. Place in a pan, completely cover with water to which you've added one cup of salt, and allow to soak overnight. Drain off the salt water and rinse thoroughly with hot water.

To make dressing, melt the butter in a heavy skillet, add the finely chopped onion and brown. The finely chopped liver of the opossum may be added if desired; it should be cooked until tender and well done. Add the bread crumbs, red pepper, Worcestershire sauce and hard-boiled egg. Salt to taste and moisten the mixture with water. Stuff the opossum, and fasten the opening with skewers or by sewing. Generously salt and pepper the outside, and place on a rack in the roasting pan. Add two or three tablespoons of water to the pan and roast in a moderate oven (350 degrees) until tender and richly brown. Baste often with the drippings while it is cooking.

Serve on a heated platter rimmed with baked sweet potatoes or yams. Follow with your favorite light dessert.

Part II

GAME BIRDS

Ducks, Geese and Upland Game Birds

Each year, approximately fifteen million ducks and geese are taken by hunters. This constitutes something like thirty million pounds of meat for the tables of American families. Some of it will arrive with its own delicate and distinctive taste, but much of it will have been soaked in wines, brines and other solutions so that you would never know you were eating a duck or goose unless you had been told. The same holds true of many upland game birds.

The Canada goose or honker is one of the grandest of all waterfowl. It has a wingspread of over five feet, and on the average will weigh from eight to ten pounds. Flying in large V formation, the thrill they awaken as they come to your decoys is truly indescribable. Their huge size makes them appear much nearer than they really are, and many an inexperienced hunter has fired at them when they were completely out of range. Canada geese are heavily coated with feathers and down, so that unless you get within range you may only wound one of these magnificent birds, leaving it to die a lingering death.

Of the duck family, the canvasback and the redhead are considered the most palatable. In the days of market hunting, a brace of either species would bring premium prices in Eastern markets. The canvasback was especially sought by epicures because of the delicate and distinctive flavor of the meat, the result of its diet of wild celery. The hunting pressure finally depleted its kind to a degree that it was necessary to ban killing them.

No species of ducks decreased more quickly than the redhead, often referred to as the "fool duck" because of its confiding disposition. This and the demand for its highly succulent flesh led to the same ban on killing it as for the canvasback.

There are two main schools of thought on how to handle duck, geese or upland game birds after the kill. Some say you should clean the bird immediately; others say it should hang and become "high" before plucking or drawing.

We won't enter into a discussion of the advantages of one argument over the other, since those who want their birds "high" think it is a sacrilege to eat them any other way, and vice versa. Those who prefer their meat "high" can't be altogether wrong, since you'll find duck and other game birds served in that state at some of the most expensive restaurants in New York, Paris and other cities. The method has been followed for centuries, so it must have its good points.

The art of hanging game birds until they become "high" involves a grave decision as the critical moment approaches. Since very often one night longer may be too long, close surveillance becomes absolutely necessary as the bird approaches the decisive stage. It must hang until the full aroma is reached, whereupon it will immediately begin to decompose. Since game birds are hung with their feathers on, you will not be greatly bothered by flies. Since a bird with a crop has a tendency to taint first in that region, the crop may be removed and doused with pepper to discourage flies. Other birds start to decompose around the vent. Either way, at the first sign of taint you must remove the feathers and draw the bird.

When it has been plucked and drawn, wash it well in salted water to which you've added some vinegar. If the bird is badly tainted, repeat the process. The final wash should be in cool, clear fresh water. Wipe dry and put inside the body a piece of charcoal, or a pulverized handful wrapped in a piece of cheesecloth, to serve as a sweetener during the cooking; but be sure to remove it before serving.

Advocates of this method say there is no gamy taste, that the meat is tender and that the flavor is incomparable. According to Fletcher Pratt and Robeson Bailey, both experts in the art of cooking, in their book *A Man and His Meals:* "A standard wild duck, the size of canvasback or mallard, should be hung from *six to twenty days or more* [the italics are mine; quick-freezing elimi- nates this necessity], depending upon the weather, then dry-plucked carefully to avoid breaking the skin. It should be drawn, wiped out with a paper towel or slightly damp cloth, a strip of bacon or salt pork deposited on the breast, and then slapped into a very hot oven. It should roast from twelve to twenty minutes without basting, the length of time depending on your taste and your oven."

Duck is a red meat, and any man who likes his meat red will truly relish one brought out rare from a fast oven. Any true epicure will think it a crime to treat this delectable bird in any other way. There are those who advise, so as to remove the gamy taste from a wild duck, soaking it overnight in a salt solution, parboiling it for a long time and stuffing it full of sauerkraut, celery or some flavor-absorbing herb. But if you have to do all this to destroy the *wild taste,* then you just don't like duck. In our opinion, to treat a duck in that way is the same thing as to take prime rib from a piece of choice beef dope it up with exotic herbs that destroy the true flavor, and then practically cremate it before taking it out of oven. If you have to do that, then you don't like the true flavor of beef.

Whether you like your birds "high," or whether you clean them as quickly as possible after the kill and then quick-freeze them for future use, I must admonish you not to try to destroy the delicate flavor of these wonderful birds. Those who don't like the flavor of duck had better stick to chicken.

ROAST DUCK   1

This method of preparing duck for the table was given to me by Francis H. Ames, the author of several outdoor books, who told me the recipe been given to him by Ted Trueblood, another noted outdoor writer. With such a recommendation, you may be certain the recipe is a good one.

1 duck per serving	Chopped apple
Celery	Salt
Chopped onion	Pepper

Clean the duck, rub with salt and pepper and stuff with mixture of chopped onion, celery and apple. Place on a rack in a baking dish, and bake at not less than 575 degrees for thirty minutes. Large ducks such as the mallard, pintail and canvasback are best for this recipe. Cooked this way, the duck remains moist, tender and slightly on the rare side.

Serve with whatever vegetable you choose. A good red wine will add zest to this tasty meal.

ROAST DUCK   2

1 duck per serving	4 cloves
1 onion per duck	Salt
2 tablespoons ground pepper	Pepper

Clean and prepare the duck for cooking as you would any fowl. Rub thoroughly inside and out with salt, pepper and ground ginger. Peel the onion, stick the four cloves into it, and put it inside the duck. Place the bird on a rack in a roasting pan and add one cup of water. Bake in a preheated oven at 325 degrees for one and a half hours, or until done. Baste often during the baking process. Test by moving the leg; if it turns freely in the joint, the duck should be done. Place on a large platter, rimmed with baked oranges (see recipe on page 138) .

Serve with mashed potatoes and green peas. For dessert we suggest jello with whipped cream.

BAKED DUCK, HUNTER'S STYLE

This recipe was given to me by a friend who makes duck his main diet during the hunting season. It will appeal especially to those who like duck on the rare side. Allow one bird per serving.

1 duck, thoroughly cleaned	1 onion, diced
¼ cup lemon juice	Salt
¼ cup Worcestershire sauce	Pepper
1 tart apple	

Blend lemon juice and Worcestershire sauce, and baste the duck thoroughly inside and out. Sprinkle with salt and pepper. Stuff with equal parts of diced onion and tart apple. Place the duck on a rack in a baking dish and bake in a preheated oven at 575 degrees. For small ducks allow 18–20 minutes, for those of medium size 20–23, and for large ducks 25 minutes.

The juice and residue in the bottom of baking dish are delicious spooned over mashed potatoes. This dish is delicious served with a good light red wine.

Creamed potatoes and a green vegetable are a good accompaniment. For dessert, serve pie or cake.

ROAST WILD DUCK

This is a variation on the foregoing recipe. For succulence, again we urge; *Do not overcook*. The meat will be rare, but until you've eaten duck served on the rare side, you have never really enjoyed the delicate flavor the bird possesses. My wife says that it should be eaten by candlelight so that people can't see the rare meat, and then everyone will enjoy it. Maybe she has a point.

1 duck per person	Salt
1 apple per duck, quartered	Pepper
2 thin slices salt pork per duck	

Place cleaned ducks on a rack in the roaster. Rub salt and pepper generously over the bird. Place slices of salt pork, two per bird, across the breast, and roast in a preheated oven at 575 degrees. The ducks should be at room temperature, and a mallard or pintail should be roasted approximately twenty to twenty-five minutes for rare, or sixteen to eighteen minutes for blood rare. Smaller ducks will require even less time.

MANDARIN DUCK

This recipe was given to us by Mrs. Lucille Scholl of Merced, California. She and her husband quite frequently fish and hunt on Topock Slough in Arizona, and it was there that we first tasted duck prepared in this way.

6 ducks (allow one per serving)	1 ounce or jigger lemon juice (fresh preferred)
1 five-ounce bottle soy sauce	1 teaspoon garlic salt
1 pound brown sugar	1 teaspoon pepper
	Sliced lemon

Clean the ducks and wipe with a damp cloth. Blend the soy sauce with equal parts of water and add sugar, lemon juice, garlic salt and pepper. Mix well to dissolve the sugar and garlic salt, and brush the ducks thoroughly inside and out with the sauce. In a 350-degree oven, bake for one and a half hours, then turn the birds and continue to bake until done. The baking dish may be garnished with lemon slices for additional seasoning if desired.

Serve on a large platter with baked oranges (see page 138), and accompanied by creamed potatoes and green peas. For dessert we suggest pie or cake with a cream sauce.

BAKED CANADA GOOSE

There are as many different ways of preparing a goose as there are of hunting it. This is a simple one which we like very much.

1 Canada goose   Pepper
Salt

Wipe the bird with a damp cloth. Salt and pepper generously inside and out. Fill with dressing, truss and place in a roasting pan, breast down. Bake in a preheated oven at 350 degrees, allowing twenty-five minutes to the pound. If it appears to be getting too brown, cover the pan with aluminum foil or a tight-fitting lid.

Cornbread Dressing

1 package commercial bread dressing	½ cup melted butter or margarine
2 cups crumbled cornbread	1 teaspoon sage
1 cup finely chopped onion	1 teaspoon marjoram
1 cup canned applesauce	1 teaspoon thyme
1 can cream of mushroom soup	

Toss lightly, and if necessary, add a little water to make the dressing moist. We like a highly seasoned dressing; if you prefer, you may omit any of the seasonings we suggest, or add some of your own favorites.

FRIED SNOW GOOSE

Since snow geese are among the smaller members of the goose family, many hunters don't try for them. When we get one, instead of plucking it as we would a larger goose, we skin and fry it as we would a quail.

1 goose, cleaned, skinned and   Cooking oil
     disjointed as you would a   Salt
     chicken for frying   Pepper
Flour

Salt, pepper and dredge all the pieces in flour. Place in a medium hot, heavy skillet to which approximately a quarter inch of cooking oil has been added. Brown thoroughly on all sides. Add approximately half a cup of water, cover and turn down the fire so that the juices barely bubble. Cook for about forty-five minutes, or until the meat is tender when tested with a fork. Add more water during cooking if necessary

Serve with fluffy steamed rice, a green vegetable, hot biscuits, and a green salad. For dessert we suggest pie or ice cream.

GOOSE BREAST

We were introduced to this unusual and delicious way of preparing the breast of goose by Lucille Scholl of California. It is one of the very few game recipes in which we use wine. The other parts of the goose may be used to make a stew with dumplings, so that none of it goes to waste.

1 or 2 goose breasts per serving   Pepper
1 cup sauterne   Garlic salt
1 cup water   Flour
Salt   Vegetable shortening

Cut the goose breast into halves and use a meat hammer to tenderize. Season with salt, pepper and garlic salt and dredge in flour. Place in a medium hot heavy skillet and brown very slowly. Mix sauterne and water, pour over the browned breast and simmer until tender.

BARBECUED QUAIL

A quail barbecue makes a fine cookout, and birds prepared this way are very tasty. You may also use grouse, since the meat is very similar.

2 birds per person	1 stick butter or margarine
1 cup barbecue sauce either your own or your favorite prepared brand	1 teaspoon Worcestershire sauce

Mix the sauce ingredients in a small stewpan and simmer for ten minutes.

Cut the birds in half, salt and pepper, and dip in barbecue sauce or brush it on thoroughly. Place the birds on a rack over a bed of charcoal, being careful not to have them too close. Cook, turning and basting frequently, until they are golden brown .The cooking time will depend upon the distance of the grill or rack from the bed of coals. This recipe serves six persons.

FRIED QUAIL

2 or 3 quails per serving	Cooking oil
Oregano	Salt
Flour	Pepper

Salt and pepper the birds, then lightly dust with oregano. Roll in flour and put into a preheated heavy skillet. Do not allow the heat to go above 325 degrees while the birds are browning. When they are brown on all sides, add a small amount of water to the skillet, cover tightly and simmer until the birds are tender, adding a little water if necessary to keep them from getting too brown.

Serve with mashed potatoes, buttered asparagus tips and fruit salad. For dessert we suggest custard pudding of your favorite flavor.

QUAIL PIE

8–10 quails, thoroughly cleaned	Flour
¼ cup cooking oil	Biscuits
4 carrots, quartered	Thyme
4 potatoes, quartered or cut into small pieces	Salt
1 onion, sliced	Pepper

Wash the quails thoroughly. Dry, salt and pepper and sprinkle lightly with thyme. Roll in flour, place in a heavy casserole and brown on all sides over a medium fire. When the birds are brown, cover them with water, add vegetables and cook until nearly done. Place the biscuits on top of the meat and vegetables and bake in a preheated oven at 400 degrees for about fifteen minutes, or until the biscuits are brown.

You will find this a welcome change from the usual method of preparing quail, and it is a complete meal in itself. For dessert, you might have jello with whipped cream. This recipe will serve four people.

QUAIL MEXICAN STYLE

This recipe was given to me by a friend who has lived in Mexico for over twenty years. He said that when his wife didn't fry quail, this was the way she always cooked it.

12 quails	½ teaspoon oregano
1 can solid pack tomatoes	2 or 3 sprigs parsley (dried may
½ teaspoon garlic powder	be used)
½ cup diced onion	Salt
1 cup washed rice	Pepper
2 green chili peppers, chopped	

Place well-washed rice in a deep, heavy skillet well oiled with bacon fat or cooking oil, along with chili peppers and onion and parsley, stirring constantly until the rice browns. Pour in the tomatoes, garlic powder, oregano, salt and pepper, and stir gently until well mixed. Add the quails, cover tightly and simmer until done, which should be in about one hour. Serve piping hot. Birds cooked this way are juicy and delicious. Serves six persons.

ROAST WILD TURKEY

Wild turkey should be roasted in very much the same way as a domestic bird. The kind of dressing you use to stuff it is optional. We like a cornbread dressing, or one with a combination of cornbread and white bread.

1 turkey, thoroughly cleaned	Pepper
Salt	Dressing of your choice

Wipe the turkey dry; rub salt and pepper over the entire bird, inside and out. Stuff with dressing as you would a domestic turkey. Place on a rack in a roasting pan, breast down, and bake in a preheated oven at 325 degrees for three and a half to four hours. If the bird is small, less time will be required. Whatever dressing you use, add two cups of applesauce instead of the liquid to moisten it.

Serve with creamed potatoes, string beans and cranberry sauce. We suggest a colorful fruit salad, followed by your choice of pie for dessert.

FRIED YOUNG WILD TURKEY

When you are hunting turkey, unless for some special reason you want a big old gobbler, try for a nice young poult and cook it this way.

1 young turkey, plucked and cleaned	Pepper
	Flour
Salt	Cooking oil

Disjoint the poult as you would a frying chicken. Salt and pepper each piece and dredge thoroughly in flour. Put cooking oil about a quarter inch deep in a heavy skillet and heat to 350 degrees. Place the turkey in the skillet, skin side down, cover tightly and cook thirty minutes, checking occasionally so as not to let it get too brown. When it is brown on both sides, check to see whether it is tender. If not, add a little water and steam a few more minutes. An hour of cooking should be ample. Make gravy with the skillet residue as you would for fried chicken.

Serve with marsh or wild rice, hot biscuits, and a salad of sliced tomatoes, onions and green peas. For dessert we suggest hot biscuits with butter and honey.

Ring-Necked Pheasant

The Chinese ring-necked pheasant is one of the most brilliantly colorful of game birds. It belongs to the same family as the domestic fowl and the peacock, and is a native of the Far East. It was not until the latter part of the nineteenth century that ring-necked pheasants were successfully introduced into the United States. The species is now common throughout much of the country, but it thrives especially in the North, West and Midwest.

Pheasants build nests directly on the ground, and lay from six to sixteen eggs. Though their insect-eating habits help the farmer, they are so prolific in some localities that they became a menace to grain fields and have had to be thinned out by permitting longer seasons and larger bag limits. In other areas, drastic steps have had to be taken to protect the pheasants from over-shooting.

The ring-necked pheasant has a very prominent white ring about the neck, and the rest of the bird is a combination of greens, crimson, purple and other colors. A cock pheasant in flight is a gorgeous sight. The hen is a mottled brown, and not nearly so colorful.

Concerning the pheasant, as concerning duck and goose, there is controversy over just when the bird should be plucked and drawn. Many connoisseurs say that it should hang by the tail feathers until they drop, and then be plucked and drawn. Connoisseurs of this school argue that a bird

hung in this way will be of better flavor, a combination of poultry and venison, and that if it is cooked at the proper time the flesh will also be tender.

We are remaining noncommital on the issue, leaving you to adhere to
whatever your custom may be, though we will say that the pheasant and the
grouse are among the tastiest of game birds.

FRIED PHEASANT

The pheasant, since it is a white-meated bird, tends to become dry when
fried. But if you cook it as you would Southern fried chicken, the meat will
remain moist and tender.

1 pheasant per person, cut up for frying as you would a chicken	Salt Pepper Flour
Butter or cooking oil (we prefer oil)	Milk

Salt and pepper each piece to taste and dredge in flour. Place in a heavy
skillet containing about a quarter of an inch of oil, cover and cook over a
medium fire until brown. Turn and brown on the other side. In the last few
minutes of cooking, remove the cover and go on frying until the pieces are
golden brown. The meat should be juicy, tender and crisp.

Remove the meat, pour off excess oil and add flour to the residue, stirring
until the flour is lightly brown. Slowly add milk, stirring constantly, until it
begins to boil lightly and the desired thickness is attained. Salt and pepper
to taste.

Serve with fluffy steamed white rice and hot biscuits. For dessert we suggest ice cream.

PHEASANT BARBECUED ON A SPIT

For a beautifully golden brown and highly tasty pheasant, we recommend this method of cooking it.

2 pheasants, cleaned and kept whole
⅓ cup melted butter or margarine
¼ cup Worcestershire sauce

½ teaspoon paprika
⅛ teaspoon Tabasco sauce
¼ teaspoon garlic powder
½ teaspoon salt

Mix together thoroughly all the above ingredients except the paprika to make a barbecue sauce. Pierce the birds with a spit, truss the legs and wings to the body and brush sauce over the whole surface, daubing a little on the inside. If time permits, let them stand for about an hour. This, though not necessary, will improve the flavor.

Just before placing on a rotisserie or in a barbecue pit, brush again with sauce. Cook over a low fire for about an hour and fifteen minutes. Sprinkle lightly with paprika and continue to cook until the birds are golden brown. If possible, use a good hardwood charcoal for the true smoke flavor.

A good rosé wine goes wonderfully with this dish.

BAKED PHEASANT IN CREAM

1 pheasant, cleaned and cut into serving pieces
½ medium-sized green pepper, cut into rings
1 tablespoon sliced pimento

1 pint half-and-half cream
Cooking oil
Salt
Pepper
Paprika

Salt, pepper and lightly flour the pheasant. Cook in a well-oiled heavy skillet until brown. Remove, place in a casserole and pour cream over all. If the pint doesn't completely cover the pieces, add canned milk diluted with water. Place the pepper rings and pimento on top and bake in a 350-degree oven until the meat is tender, or approximately one hour.

Serve with mashed potatoes, green peas, and fruit salad.

BROILED PHEASANT

Cooked this way, one pheasant can serve two people; but for hearty eaters, allow one bird per person. You'll find it as juicy and tasty as anything you ever ate.

1 or 2 pheasants	Salt
Butter or margarine	Pepper

Cut the pheasant in halves lengthwise. Brush on melted butter or margarine, inside and out, and rub with salt and pepper. Place under the broiler and brown on both sides. Remove from the broiler, turn the heat down to 325 degrees, and again brush the birds thoroughly with butter. Wrap each half separately, completely sealing the edges. Place on a cookie sheet or large pan, and bake in the oven for approximately an hour, depending upon the size of the bird.

Serve with steamed, fluffy buttered rice and a green vegetable.

Sage Grouse

The sage grouse, sometimes called the spiny-tailed pheasant, is the largest of North American grouse, and the most magnificent of all Western game birds. It's not as gaudy and colorful as the ring-necked pheasant, but when a large cock takes off from under your feet you will stand momentarily spellbound. Lumbering away in flight, it may remind you of an overloaded bomber struggling for altitude; but it quickly gains speed, and while you stand in awe at the size of the bird it will already be out of range. The hen of the species will weigh from one and a half to three and a half pounds, the cock sometimes as much as seven pounds.

Grasshoppers and other insects and alfalfa are among their main foods, but sage is the winter diet of this grouse. For all upland game birds, we recommend drawing as soon as is practical after the kill, but especially so with the sage grouse. Some hunters disdain the bird, saying it has too strong a flavor of sage. But we have eaten it many times, and have yet to find one that did—perhaps because we always draw the bird soon after the kill.

SAGE GROUSE SMOTHERED

2 sage grouse (will serve four to six persons)	Salt
	Pepper
3 tablespoons cooking oil	Parsley flakes
1 quart half-and-half cream	

Cut the grouse into serving pieces, wash and dry with a towel. Salt, pepper, dredge with flour and place in a pan containing the cooking oil. Over medium heat brown all the pieces. Then transfer them to a baking dish, arranging them as close together as possible, and in a single layer. Pour cream over all the pieces, sprinkle them generously with parsley flakes and bake in a preheated oven at 325 degrees for two hours.

Check after one hour to make sure that the meat is not sticking to the bottom of the pan. Then cover tightly with a lid or a closely fitted sheet of aluminum foil, and bake for another hour.

Serve with a casserole of brown rice and hot biscuits. For a salad, we suggest lime jello with shredded carrot, green pepper and olives, followed by a dessert of homemade peppermint ice cream.

Dove

In the Southwest there are two commonly hunted species of dove, the mourning dove, and the larger white-winged dove. The latter is the more highly prized of the two, mainly on account of its size, which is half again that of the mourning dove. As the name suggests, the white on each wing is easily seen, both in flight and when the bird is roosting. At the first sign of chilly weather or fall storms, white-winged doves start their migration to Mexico, where the weather is warmer in winter than in our Southwest.

The hunting of doves is banned in nineteen of our states, but in those areas with a large dove population, hunting them is considered the sportiest of all wing shooting. On the first day of the season it isn't difficult to get your limit. But by the second or third day the birds will have become exceedingly wary, and their flight paths, normally straight and level with little variation, will have become very erratic, with constant changes of altitude and direction. To look down the gun barrel and find your bird is almost impossible, and hitting it is still more difficult. Doves quickly become suspicious of the slightest movement, or of any new object that crosses their flight paths. By the second or third day they have become such a difficult target that it is doubtful whether an average hunter will get six birds per box of shells.

Not that I mean to belittle the pheasant hunter, but I have seen more than one of them return to the car with a dazed expression on his face and completely flabbergasted at not being able to hit the bird, and will confess it is a far more difficult target than the pheasant. After a season of dove hunting, drop in on a pheasant hunt and notice the difference. As you sight down the gun barrel at the pheasant, a large bird as compared to the tiny dove, it will look as though you are drawing a bead on a B-52 bomber that is barely moving.

The best time to hunt doves is late in the afternoon or early in the morning, as they fly out to their feeding grounds. You may get in a blind near the field they are feeding in, or select a good spot directly under the flight path, which as a rule is consistent until extreme hunting pressure makes them change. If you are under their flight path, you will get shooting as they return to their roosting or resting place. If you are properly located, you should get your limit without moving out of your blind except to retrieve a downed bird. For dove hunting I prefer a 20-gauge shotgun with a low-base shell and No. 8 shot. This load, which you can shoot all day without suffering a bruised shoulder, is ample to bring down so small a bird.

There are numerous ways of preparing doves for cooking. Many hunters tear the breast loose and bring home only that portion—a fast and easy way to clean them, and one from which you take home the best part of the bird. But being of the old school, I prefer to dry-pluck mine and cook the whole bird, saving even the tiny heart, liver and gizzard for gravy. The meat is dark in color and fine in texture, with a taste similar to that of a well-prepared duck. The meat is less dry than that of most white-meated birds, and I prefer it to the more popular quail.

BAKED MOURNING OR WHITE-WINGED DOVE

2 or 3 doves per serving	Marjoram
Salt	Cooking oil
Pepper	½ cup applesauce per serving
Oregano	

After the doves have been thoroughly cleaned, sprinkle lightly with salt, pepper, oregano and marjoram. Place in a heavy skillet and brown in a small amount of cooking oil.

Remove from the skillet and prepare a moist cornbread dressing, using applesauce in place of water. Spread a layer of dressing in a baking pan and place the birds on top, in such a manner that there will be only one layer. Place the rest of the dressing around or over the birds. Cover the dish with aluminum foil and bake in a preheated oven at 300 degrees for forty-five minutes. Test the birds with a fork; if they are not tender, bake a little longer.

Serve with buttered asparagus tips, yams and a pineapple-cream cheese salad, with lemon pie for dessert.

FRIED MOURNING OR WHITE-WINGED DOVE

3 birds per serving (more for hearty eaters)	Cooking oil
	Flour
1 teaspoon Worcestershire sauce	Salt
	Pepper

These birds are better if they are plucked, not skinned, and if the whole bird and not just the breast is used. This way, they not only are more moist but have a better flavor. When they have been thoroughly cleaned, wipe them dry, salt and pepper and dredge in flour. Place approximately a quarter inch of cooking oil in a heavy skillet and heat it to 350 degrees. Place the doves in the skillet and brown on all sides. Add Worcestershire sauce and enough water to make the liquid about half an inch deep. Cover with a tight-fitting lid and simmer about thirty minutes, or until tender. Remove the doves, stir two teaspoons of flour into one cup of water, and pour this into the skillet to make gravy. Stir constantly until it is done.

Serve with fluffy steamed rice, green beans, hot biscuits, and a salad of lettuce, cucumber and tomatoes. For dessert we suggest spice cake or fresh fruit slices.

DOVE POT PIE

10 doves, cleaned	1 small green pepper
3 carrots	1 tablespoon Worcestershire sauce
3 medium-sized potatoes	
1 small can string beans	Cooking oil
6 green onions	Salt
½ teaspoon sweet basil	Pepper
1 can of ten biscuits, or make your own	Oregano

Salt and pepper the doves generously, sprinkle with oregano and dredge in flour. Sear on all sides in a heavy skillet over a medium fire, cooking for about fifteen minutes. Add Worcestershire sauce and onions. Before the onions are brown, pour in enough water to cover the birds, and add sweet basil and green pepper cut into shreds. Then cover and simmer for forty-five minutes.

Prepare the rest of the vegetables by cutting them into bite-sized pieces, add to the pot and cook fifteen minutes. Place the biscuits on top, moistening them on each side with the juice in the pot. Bake in a preheated oven at 375 degrees until the biscuits are browned.

Ten birds will serve four hungry people, and you will have a complete meal in the one pot.

LA PALOMA MEXICO
(Dove, Mexican Style)

When you tire of eating dove fried or baked, try this spicy way of cooking it.

6 doves (three each for two hearty eaters)	¼ teaspoon garlic powder
	¼ teaspoon marjoram
2 tablespoons cooking oil	¼ teaspoon oregano
1 small can tomato sauce	⅛ teaspoon cumin
½ cup diced onion	Water
2 ounces green chilies chopped	Worcestershire sauce

Clean the doves thoroughly, salt, pepper and roll in flour. Brown in a heavy skillet to which you have added a little cooking oil. Add the onions and a dash of Worcestershire sauce and cook two minutes, stirring constantly. Now add the rest of the ingredients and enough water to cover the birds. Cover and simmer for one and a half to two hours.

Serve with brown or white rice and a green vegetable. As a rule, dove cooked this way is so tender that the meat falls off the bone.

Band-Tailed Pigeon

The band-tailed pigeon is found only along the Pacific coast, except for a few in Arizona and New Mexico. The few times I've hunted it were in southern California, where the birds seemed to inhabit the most inaccessible places. You can expect to have to hunt them under extremely difficult conditions—for example, at the top of a heavily timbered mountain, where it is impossible to see a bird wing its way in until it is directly overhead, flying very high and extremely fast. It may be out of sight before you can fire a shot, and most of those you do fire are likely to be misses.

Band-tailed pigeons should be dry-plucked and drawn soon as possible after the kill. The meat is like that of the dove, but according to my experience the band-tailed pigeon is more likely to be tough. If you think what you have is an old bird, cook it in such a manner as to make it tender.

BROILED OR BARBECUED PIGEON

Young pigeons will be tender, and are excellent broiled or cooked over charcoal. Cooking over charcoal may take a little longer than broiling.

2 pigeons per person for hearty eaters	Salt
¼ pound butter, for four pigeons	Pepper
2 tablespoons wine vinegar or red wine for each quarter pound of butter	Thyme

Melt the butter, mix all the seasonings, and add salt and pepper to taste. If only one quarter pound of butter is used, just a pinch of thyme will be sufficient. Keep the mixture just warm enough so that the butter will not solidify. Split the birds in half lengthwise and place them in a broiler pan covered with foil. Brush the basting mixture over them thoroughly and place under the broiler for eight to ten minutes. When lightly brown, turn and baste; then broil for eight minutes more. The birds should be just right by then; if not, cook a little longer but don't overcook.

With pigeons cooked in this way we prefer a good red wine served at room temperature.

PIGEON POT PIE

4 pigeons, cleaned and disjointed	Bacon grease
	Salt
3 carrots, diced	Pepper
2 potatoes, cubed	Flour
1 large onion, chopped	Biscuit dough
¼ pound margarine or butter	Boiling water

Cut up the pigeon, sprinkle with salt, pepper and flour and brown lightly in bacon grease. Cover with boiling water, add vegetables and simmer for thirty minutes. Add margarine or butter and arrange biscuits to cover the top. (Canned biscuits may be used.) Place in a preheated oven at 400 degrees and bake until the biscuits are browned.

As an accompaniment we suggest a fruit salad.

This will serve four persons.

SMOTHERED PIGEON

This is a good recipe for those pigeons you suspect may be on the tough side.

1 pigeon for each person (more for hearty eaters)	1 medium onion, peeled and sliced
Salt	Cooking oil
Pepper	1 tablespoon Worcestershire sauce
Flour	

Cut the birds in halves lengthwise through the back and breast. Salt and pepper them, dredge in flour and lightly brown on both sides in a heavy skillet over a medium fire. Add water to a depth of about one inch in the skillet. Stir in Worcestershire sauce, and add onion. Cover with a close-fitting lid and simmer for about one hour, or until the birds are tender. Remove, make a flour paste by stirring a tablespoon of flour into a cup of water, and add to the residue in the skillet to make gravy. Cook and thin to the desired consistency.

Serve with fluffy white rice, a green vegetable, hot biscuits and a tossed salad if desired. For dessert we suggest apple pie.

Part III

GAME FISH

How to Care for Fish

Of all game, fish are sought after by more people than any other. With so many millions who go fishing, it is impossible to estimate the amount of edible fish caught annually, though it probably runs into the millions of tons. As with deer and other game, much of the fish taken is lost as a result of not knowing or adhering to a few simple rules, and much of what reaches the table is not in its most palatable form. Since no other food deteriorates so quickly as fish, a few simple rules on how to clean and care for it can make all the difference in its quality, and allow you to enjoy fish as never before.

It is seldom possible to buy ocean fish that will compare in taste with fresh-water fish, newly caught and properly cared for. Much of the salt-water fish in the markets has been caught days away from shore, and has remained in the ship's hold for a long period of time, often poorly refrigerated and many times not gutted. Such fish naturally reaches the market in the first stages of deterioration, and is no longer fit for human consumption. Properly cared for, fish will not have the strong odor that so often arises from ocean fish as it is being cooked and served.

A wading trout fisherman should clean each trout immediately, placing it in a creel on a bed of damp moss or grass so that air may circulate around it freely. Immediate cleaning ensures that the fish will bleed thoroughly as it should. Fish caught from a boat or from the shore may be kept alive on a stringer or in a live box until they are cleaned. Then they should immediately be placed in the refrigerator or on ice. It is important to keep the fish alive until it is to be cleaned, so that it will be properly bled.

We prefer to skin all larger fish, so as to eliminate the possibility of having the skin impart a strong flavor to the fish—though some people seem to prefer that flavor.

111

How to Clean and Fillet a Fish
in Three Minutes

To clean and fillet a four- or five-pound bass in three minutes with seven strokes of the knife seems an incredible feat to many, but with a good knife and a pair of pliers it can be done easily. The knife should have a fairly stiff ten-inch blade; fish-skinning pliers are available at most sporting goods stores for about a dollar a pair (Fig. 1).

Follow these simple step-by-step instructions and you'll discover, to your amazement, that cleaning fish need not be the disagreeable chore it is when you scale and gut the fish. With this method you can clean fish in the kitchen without making a mess of scales and remnants. Also, removing the skin improves the flavor of the fish, unless you are among those who prefer the strong flavor imparted by the skin.

To begin, place the fish on a cleaning board, and with an old towel or cloth, hold the head with the left hand (Fig. 2). The cloth serves two purposes: to protect your hand if the knife slips and to help you to hold the fish securely. Place the knife blade at about a 45-degree angle and start to cut toward the gill plate. As soon as the cut is started, keep the knife level and cut along the backbone to the gill plate (Fig. 3). If the fish is large, a slight sawing action as you cut through the rib bones may be necessary. When you have reached the gill plate, stop (Fig. 4). Turn the fish over and repeat the operation on the other side. At this stage of the cleaning process, sever the head (Fig. 5). You can now discard the head, backbone and intestines, which are intact.

To remove the skin from the two slabs of meat, place the fish on the cleaning board, flesh side up. Grasp the tail with the pliers. Holding the knife at a slight angle (Fig. 6), use a sawing motion and cut toward the head. Thus, with one fast operation you have removed the skin from the fillet (Fig. 7). Repeat the same operation on the other slab of meat.

Now, the last and final operation is to remove the bones and the belly meat, leaving you with a boneless piece of fish. Place the skinned slab of meat on the cleaning board. Place the knife at the severed end of the ribs (Fig. 8) and with one cutting motion, cut out the bones and belly meat. If you prefer, you may remove the dorsal fin from the backbone and cook this portion, which contains a lot of meat.

With seven strokes of the knife, and in approximately three minutes, you have completely cleaned your fish, giving you two boneless and firm-meated fillets—all with no mess and no fuss. Try this simple, easy way of cleaning your fish. With a little practice, you'll soon become quite proficient, and it will give you a different outlook on this phase of your fishing trips.

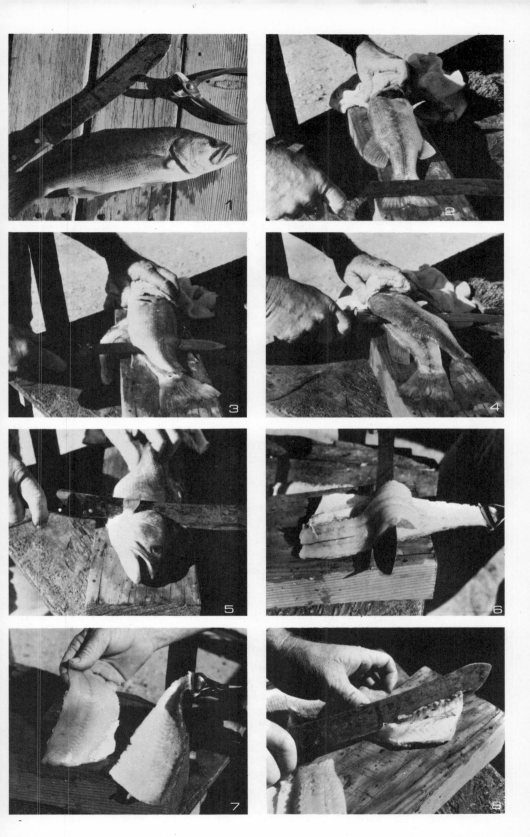

FISH FRIED IN DEEP FAT

Fish fried this way is practically grease-free and really tasty. But be sure all the bones are removed when you fillet the fish.

2 pounds fish fillets	Corn meal
1 egg	1 tablespoon salt
2 cups milk, fresh or canned	Salt
Cooking oil	Pepper

Break the egg into the milk and add salt and pepper. With an egg beater, thoroughly mix all ingredients, making sure to dissolve the salt completely. Dip the fish into this mixture, roll in corn meal and drop into a heavy kettle of deep fat preheated to 375-400 degrees. Add the fish slowly, so as not to lower the temperature. When it is golden brown, lift it from the fat and drain it as you would French-fries or doughnuts. Keep the pieces small enough so as to cook quickly—and keep the fat hot, or the fish will be grease-soaked and soggy. Serve on a large platter garnished with slices of sweet onion, lemon wedges and parsley.

Serve with hashed brown potatoes and coleslaw.

This will feed four hearty eaters.

BAKED STRIPED BASS

This unusual way of handling and preparing bass was given to me by Robeson Bailey, author of numerous articles in outdoor magazines as well as co-author of *A Man and His Meals.*

The first requisite is an ice chest large enough and efficient enough to hold a day's catch and keep it cold. Immediately upon catching a fish, place it in the ice chest, *ungutted and unscaled.* When you get home, rinse the fish in *ice water,* wrap each fish singly in plastic or foil and QUICK FREEZE. Keep the fish stored at zero or colder until it is to be used. When you're ready for a fish dinner, follow these simple instructions.

1 bass of average size (three to four pounds) per two persons	Salt
1 tablespoon dry white wine	Pepper
Lemon juice	Butter

Remove the fish from the freezer, then when it is about half thawed—and not until then—scale it and remove the guts. If it is large, split it in half lengthwise and place it on foil, flesh side up. Be sure the foil is large enough to wrap and seal securely. Brush on lemon juice, dot generously with butter, sprinkle with salt and pepper, add one tablespoon of the wine to each wrapping, and seal as nearly airtight as possible. Bake in a preheated oven at 400 degrees for about one hour, or until fish are done, depending upon the size of the fish.

As you unwrap the foil, be prepared for an aroma that will really excite the taste buds. This recipe can be used for any fish that is suitable for baking.

Serve on a platter garnished with lemon wedges and parsley or watercress.

BROILED FISH

This appetizing way of preparing fish is suitable for either fresh- or salt-water bass, as well as catfish.

One two- or three-pound fish	**Butter**
(will make two servings)	**Salt**
Lemon juice, preferably fresh	**Pepper**
Soy sauce	

Wash and clean the fish thoroughly, and cut it in half lengthwise along the backbone. Cut off the head at the gill plate and place the halves, skin down, on broiler tray lined with aluminum foil. Brush thoroughly with lemon juice. Blend the soy sauce, melted butter, salt and pepper and brush on the fish. Broil for about fifteen minutes, during which extra sauce may be added if desired; do not turn the fish. When it is done, place on a large plate with a garnish of lemon wedges and parsley. Sweet pickles and any fish sauce you choose may be served as condiments.

FRIED FISH MARINATED IN BEER

Although we don't recommend marinating game in wine, beer or fancy sauces, some people think marinating fish in beer adds to the flavor. We suggest that you try it and form your own opinion. Certainly it doesn't make the fish any less palatable.

2 or 3 pounds fish fillets	**Pepper**
Corn meal	**2 cans beer**
Salt	

Pour the beer into a large bowl, add the fish and let it stand for approximately two hours. Remove, drain, salt and pepper and roll in corn meal. Place in a heavy skillet in fairly deep fat and fry until golden brown. Remove and drain on an absorbent towel or paper. Serve on a large platter, garnished with lemon wedges, sliced onion and parsley.

Serve with pinto beans and coleslaw. Sweet pickles are an excellent condiment with fried fish.

FRIED FISH, SOUTHERN STYLE

Either fresh- or salt-water species may be cooked in this way. Larger fish such as the catfish, black bass and salt-water species belonging to the bass family are all better skinned and cut into fillets.

4–5 pounds filleted fish	Garlic salt (optional)
Salt	Celery salt (optional)
Pepper	Cooking oil
Corn meal	

After the fish have been cleaned and filleted, cut into pieces of the desired size, salt and pepper, and roll in corn meal. Put into a heavy skillet or Dutch oven something between a half inch and an inch of cooking oil, and heat it to between 375 and 400 degrees. Add the fish in such a way that the pieces are not on top of each other. Do this slowly, so as to avoid causing the temperature to drop. Fry to a golden brown (approximately eight to ten minutes on each side). Turn the fish with long-handled tongs, being careful not to tear the pieces apart. Drain on a paper towel or absorbent cloth.

Serve piping hot, on a large platter garnished with slices of lemon and parsley. Accompany it with pinto beans, hushpuppies, tomato hot sauce (see recipe on page 143), and coleslaw. Other condiments, such as horseradish and pickles, may be served with meal if desired.

BAKED STUFFED FISH

A good baked fish is a welcome change from frying. This recipe, given us by a friend in Florida, is the best we've tried.

1 three- to five-pound fish, cleaned and split	1½ cups diced celery
8 slices bread	½ cup diced onion
1 stick (¼ pound) butter or margarine	3 or 4 slices salt pork

Wash and drain the fish. The backbone may be removed if desired, but this is not necessary. Toast the bread lightly and let it cool. Melt the butter, add celery and onions and simmer until tender. Break or cut the toast into small pieces in a large bowl, toss thoroughly with a fork, and slowly add onion, celery and butter mixture in the process. Salt the fish, adding a little pepper if desired. Lay one half, skin down, on an oiled baking dish, and spread the stuffing over it. Score the other half of the fish and lay it on top. Cover the stuffing that falls from under the top half with aluminum foil. Lay three or four strips of salt pork over the fish, and bake in a preheated oven at 350 degrees for about an hour. In the last ten minutes of baking, remove the foil so that the stuffing will brown.

If you want to make this a really fancy dish, fifteen minutes before the fish is done, open a can of mushroom soup, stir it and pour it over the fish, and return to the oven to finish baking.

This should serve four people.

BAKED FISH

This is our favorite recipe for fish caught in the Gulf of Mexico—such as red fish, snapper, pompano and other members of the bass family.

1 four- or five-pound fish, cleaned thoroughly, with skin left on	½ cup bread crumbs
	1 tablespoon Worcestershire sauce
½ teaspoon dry mustard	1 cup water
1 package sour cream mix	Salt
2 lemons, juiced	Pepper

Cut the fish in halves lengthwise and place flesh side up on a large sheet of aluminum foil. Brush on lemon juice, salt and pepper, fold the edges of the foil to seal securely and bake in a 350-degree oven for thirty minutes. While the fish is baking, mix sour cream according to directions, add dry mustard, Worcestershire sauce and a tablespoon of lemon juice, and mix thoroughly. Remove the fish from the oven, spread evenly with the sauce, and sprinkle with bread crumbs. With the foil open, return it to the oven for about fifteen minutes, or until the bread crumbs are brown and the sauce is thoroughly warmed. Serve on a large platter garnished with lemon slices and parsley.

French-fried potatoes and a salad of lettuce wedges will go well with this dish.

The recipe serves six persons.

FISH CHOWDER

For making chowder we prefer whitefish, but you can use any other available fish. A good chowder is a meal in itself.

1½ pounds fish, preferably Rocky Mountain whitefish or some member of the bass family
2 bay leaves, crushed
½ teaspoon dried sweet basil leaves
4 strips bacon
4 medium-sized potatoes, diced
1 medium-sized onion, diced
1 tablespoon Worcestershire sauce
2 tablespoons butter or margarine
3 cups milk
Pepper
Salt
Celery salt

Cut the fish into thirds if necessary, and place in a pot of cold water. Add the pepper and the sweet basil. Place on the fire, bring to a boil and simmer for approximately ten minutes. Remove the fish and let it cool. Then, with your fingers, remove all the meat from the bones and place it in a dish.

Dice or cut the bacon into small pieces and fry until crisp. Add the onion and brown lightly, then add the potatoes and completely cover with water. Add salt, celery salt and pepper to taste, and cook until the potatoes are soft. Mash some of the potatoes with a fork and cook down until thick, stirring frequently so they won't burn. Add the fish and the milk; heat but do not boil. Remove from the fire, add butter or margarine and Worcestershire sauce and serve piping hot. A good green salad and garlic French bread or crackers go well with chowder. The recipe serves four persons.

TROUT LOAF

This dish is similar to salmon loaf, and equally good.

1 quart canned trout	2 hard-boiled eggs, diced
2 eggs	½ teaspoon pepper, coarsely
10 crackers, crushed	ground if possible
1 teaspoon dried sweet basil	1 small can tomato sauce
leaves, crushed	1 teaspoon Worcestershire
½ cup canned milk	sauce

Carefully remove from the trout the skin and any large bones that have not softened in the canning process. Mix thoroughly with the crackers first, then add basil, milk, hard-boiled eggs and pepper. Place in a baking dish and press the mixture to an even height, so that it is not rounded. Mix Worcestershire and tomato sauces together and pour evenly over the top. Bake forty-five minutes in a preheated oven at 350 degrees. Do not let the loaf become too dry; if necessary, add a little water from time to time.

Serve with potatoes au gratin or macaroni and cheese, green peas, and a salad of canned pear halves and grated Longhorn cheese, sprinkled with paprika. For dessert we suggest your choice of pie.

TROUT CROQUETTES

Here is a quick and easily prepared meal that the whole family will enjoy.

1 pint canned trout	½ teaspoon parsley flakes,
1 egg	crushed
¼ cup canned milk	¼ teaspoon pepper
	½ cup crushed cornflakes

Remove from the trout the skin and any large bones that have not softened in the canning process. Add the egg, milk and seasonings and mix thoroughly. Shape into small patties, roll in cornflake crumbs and fry in a well-oiled heavy skillet over a medium fire until golden brown. No salt is usually necessary, since there should be enough in the fish from the canning process. When the patties are golden brown, serve on a large platter garnished with lemon wedges and parsley.

Green string beans and a tossed green salad make a good accompaniment, followed by peach or apple cobbler with cream.

This recipe should serve two hungry people.

TROUT COCKTAIL

This makes a very tasty appetizer, and is a good way of using whatever trout you may have frozen. If you have more meat than is needed, simply place it in a plastic bag and drop it back into the freezer for future use.

1 trout, approximately sixteen inches long, or two or three smaller ones
1 teaspoon salt
½ teaspoon pepper
3 bay leaves, crushed
¼ teaspoon thyme
¼ teaspoon Worcestershire sauce

If the trout is large, cut it into thirds. Place in a stew kettle and completely cover with water. Add the seasonings and boil for ten minutes; then remove from the fire and leave the fish to cool in the broth so as to absorb the seasonings. With your fingers, carefully remove the meat and skin from the bones. Arrange the flaked meat in cocktail glasses, approximately two tablespoons to a serving, and place in the refrigerator to cool. Just before serving, cover the meat with a cocktail sauce, such as you would use for a whitefish cocktail.

This should make four to six servings.

TROUT CASSEROLE

1 pint canned trout
1 can Cheddar cheese soup
1½ cans water (using soup can to measure)
1½ cups minute rice
½ medium-sized green pepper, cut into rings
6 green onions, chopped
Salt
Pepper

Place soup in a stew pan and add water, a little at a time, stirring so that the soup will be free of lumps. Add green pepper rings and onion. Heat over a low fire, stirring constantly, until the mixture comes to a boil. Remove from fire. Remove skin from the canned trout and break into small chunks in a casserole. Add rice, salt and pepper to taste, and mix well. Cover this with the flavored cheese soup, mixing lightly. Place in a 350-degree oven and bake twenty-five minutes. There should be moisture on the top, not all of it having been absorbed by the rice.

Serve with lemon wedges. Summer squash and a salad of romaine lettuce with your favorite dressing are a good acccompaniment. For dessert we suggest pineapple sherbet. The recipe serves two or three persons.

TROUT À LA STURDIVANT

This is one my favorite ways of preparing trout during a camping trip, but it works just as well at home.

2 trout per person (more if they are small)	Corn meal
	One or two slices bacon per fish
Salt	Garlic salt (optional)
Pepper	Celery salt (optional)

Wash and clean the trout thoroughly, and remove the head. Season with salt and pepper, adding garlic and celery salt if desired. Roll in corn meal, or sprinkle with it. If fish are small, wrap one or two strips of bacon around each one; otherwise lay two strips lengthwise along each one. To cook over open coals, double wrap in aluminum foil, sealing thoroughly with a drugstore wrap, and place on a bed of glowing coals. After fifteen or twenty minutes, turn and cook for fifteen or twenty minutes more. To cook at home, use only one layer of foil, and bake in a preheated oven at approximately 425 degrees.

As you open the foil, breathe deeply. The aroma should not be missed!

Serve with scalloped potatoes or sweet corn and spinach. In place of salad, we suggest lemon jello. Old-fashioned bread pudding makes a good dessert to end this meal.

SMOKED TROUT

There are numerous ways of smoking fish, and though I do not insist that this is the best, it is one of the simplest. Fish smoked according to this recipe will keep for an indefinite length of time.

Using freshly caught fish, clean thoroughly and wipe dry. With a butcher knife, cut lengthwise along the backbone, working from the tail toward the head. Upon reaching the gill plate, sever the head. The trout will now be cut in half.

After all the fish you plan to smoke have been cut in this fashion, place them on a table with the meat side up. Sprinkle liberally with salt and pepper. Use a lot of pepper if you like fish highly seasoned. Place the fish in a cool, dry, shady place and let it stand for several hours. The salt will help to dehydrate it. Place the fish in a smoker; if it is one designed for hanging the fish, hang them with the thick end down; and if they are to be laid on racks, place them with the meat side up.

For smoking we prefer to use Western mesquite or, if possible, the wood of some nut tree such as hickory or pecan. If none of these is available, we use quaking aspen. We usually smoke trout from thirty-six to forty-eight hours, depending both upon the amount of heat used and upon the size of the trout. But it is the smoking, not the heat, that cures the trout and gives them the true smoke flavor. During the last few hours it is permissible to increase the heat, but it should be checked occasionally so as to avoid overcooking the fish.

If you plan to keep smoked trout for any length of time, it is best to seal them in fruit jars under pressure. Cut the smoked fish crosswise and place in fruit jar. Pour one-fourth cup of cooking oil (preferably peanut oil) over each pint of fish, tighten the lid and place in a pressure cooker. Cook for forty-five minutes at ten pounds' pressure, to ensure that the fish are well done. Smoked fish prepared in this way will retain its delicious flavor for practically an unlimited time. Open it as you desire, for example as hors d'oeuvres for a game dinner.

Note: This recipe may be used for any good fish with a high oil content—whitefish, salmon, mullet or even catfish.

SMOKED TROUT

Here is another smoked trout recipe, one that is used quite often by many fish smokers. Note that no pepper is used in this recipe.

Salt, fine grind   Garlic Salt
Brown sugar   Celery Salt

Split the fish down the backbone. Mix equal parts of salt and brown sugar and sprinkle heavily. Let stand for eight hours, then rinse in cold water.

Place the fish on wire meat racks or hang from a nail in a smoker. If wire mesh is used, place fish skin side down. For wood, use dry alder, cottonwood, maple, aspen or any good hardwood from which the bark has been removed. Do not let temperature go above 150 degrees. After about twenty-four hours, check and see if the fish seems done; if not keep in smoker a little longer.

Store the fish so that air can circulate freely around them.

SMOKED SALMON

Every salmon fisherman has his own pet theory on how to smoke or can salmon. This is a very popular recipe in the Northwest.

Coarse salt   Garlic salt (optional
Pepper

Split the salmon down the back and remove the backbone. Salt with medium coarse salt and let stand twelve to sixteen hours.

Wash or rinse thoroughly in cold water, wipe dry and add pepper and garlic salt to taste. Cut into chunks about two or three inches long and three-quarters to one inch thick. Place in smoker for approximately forty-eight hours, never letting temperature rise above 150 degrees. An oven thermometer is almost a necessity. Use aspen, alder, or any hardwood for fuel.

How to Can Trout

Our object in telling how to can trout isn't to promote hoarding, or to help you become a fish hog. It is merely a suggestion as a way to keep fish for later use in croquettes, fish loaf or numerous other recipes, as you would use salmon.

Be sure to check with the game department of the state where you fish, to make sure what the legal limit is. Most states set a legal limit upon the quantity you may have in possession, and you will not want to exceed it.

Trout of any size may be used for canning, but the results are much better if they are at least twelve inches long. After removing the entrails, be sure to remove the blood from the vein along the backbone, and rinse the fish until it is thoroughly clean. Remove the head and slice the fish in crosswise pieces approximately two inches long. Pack pint jars as tightly as you can, but be careful not to fill above the curve of the neck. To each pint jar add half a teaspoon of salt. Seal as tightly as possible and cook in a pressure cooker for ninety minutes at a pressure of fifteen pounds. Reduce the pressure to zero before attempting to remove the lid. Remove the jars and cool according to the directions accompanying the pressure cooker.

As a safety measure, all canning recipes recommend that pressurized fish be recooked before eating.

FRIED FROG LEGS

Frog legs are truly a dish for epicures, and this recipe will delight the most fastidious.

8 pairs frog legs (hind legs only)	Cracker crumbs
½ cup lemon juice	Salt
1 egg	Pepper

Skin the frog legs and place them in boiling water to which you've added the salt and lemon juice. Boil or scald for about two minutes, remove and wipe dry. Beat the egg lightly and dip the legs in it, then roll them in cracker crumbs. Fry in deep fat until golden brown or until done; this should be three to five minutes, depending upon the size of the legs.

Serve with buttered steamed rice, a green vegetable and hot biscuits. For dessert, we suggest jello with a dab of whipped cream, or ice cream of your favorite flavor.

BAKED FROG LEGS

This way of preparing frog legs will please the most fastidious. If the frogs are young ones, the meat will all but melt in your mouth.

2 to 4 pairs frog legs per person, depending upon size	Seasoning salt
¼ pound butter or margarine, per four persons	Milk
	Cornflake crumbs

Cover a shallow baking dish or cookie sheet with aluminum foil, turning the edges up about one inch to form a shallow rim. Dip frog legs in milk, sprinkle with seasoning salt, and roll in cornflake crumbs. Place in a single layer on aluminum foil with the melted butter or margarine. Bake in a pre-heated oven at 350 degrees for twenty minutes; turn and bake twenty minutes more, or until tender.

Serve with fluffy steamed and buttered rice, zucchini, hot biscuits, and a salad of sliced tomatoes.

FRIED FROG LEGS, TOPOCK MARSH STYLE

Topock Marsh, Arizona's largest swamp is densely populated with frogs as well as ducks, geese, largemouth bass and other fresh-water fish. We have spent much time hunting and fishing in that area. The frogs there are not as large as in the South, but as firm believers in the old Scottish precept, "Cook all edible food and waste naught," we even save the front legs of the frogs. Two front legs are equivalent to one hind leg, and are just as delicious.

3 pairs frog legs per person   **Salt**
Flour   **Pepper**
Shortening

Frog legs are among the very few game dishes that we recommend soaking in salt water. Keep them in a brine solution for approximately two hours. Remove, wipe dry, salt and pepper to taste and dust freely with flour. Place in a moderately hot skillet containing about a quarter inch of shortening, and lightly brown. Frogs' legs are very tender unless you happen to have caught an old one. If they appear tough, add a little water to the skillet, cover and let them simmer a few minutes until tender. Make a cream gravy with the residue in the skillet, as you would for fried chicken or any other fowl.

Serve with fluffy steamed rice and hot biscuits, with a pineapple and cream cheese salad, and jello for dessert.

How to Clean and Cook Crayfish

Place the crayfish in a tub of clear water and leave them overnight. This is a very cannibalistic crustacean, and no doubt some will have devoured their fellow crayfish by morning. Fill a large stew pot with water and add three bay leaves, a teaspoon of peppercorns, one-fourth cup of salt and a teaspoon of caraway seed. Bring to a rolling boil and drop in live crayfish. Cook for six to eight minutes, or until they turn bright red. Drain the crayfish. When they are cool enough to handle, break off the tails and peel, removing the intestinal tract and the gall cyst, which is bitter, at the same time. With a little practice you will learn to do this with a single jerk.

CRAYFISH GUMBO

1 pound crayfish, cooked and cleaned
½ cup salt pork, cut into small chunks
1 onion, diced
½ pound okra
1 No. 303 can tomatoes
1 tablespoon parsley flakes
1 can kernel corn, drained
¼ teaspoon cayenne pepper
2 cups hot water
1 pint half-and-half cream
Salt
Pepper

Fry salt pork until light brown. Add onions and cook five minutes, stirring often. Add okra, tomatoes, corn, seasonings and hot water and cook until okra is tender. Add cream and crayfish, bring just to a simmer and serve piping hot.

CRAYFISH COCKTAIL

To make a huge success of a game dinner, after having served your guests with smoked trout, smoked venison sausage and other tasty tidbits as hors d'oeuvres, place this tasty cocktail before them to start the meal.

4 or 5 crayfish per cocktail,   Cocktail sauce
depending upon size

Cook the crayfish as directed above. Break off the tails and peel, removing the intestinal tract at the same time. Put in cocktail glass, cool in refrigerator and just before serving add a tablespoon of cocktail sauce to each serving (see recipes for cocktail sauce on page 143).

FRIED CRAYFISH TAILS

In my youth one of the highlights a weekend was to clean and cook a mess of crawdads right on the bank of the stream where I had caught them. It is surprising to me that more people don't eat crayfish. They are among the most delicious of crustaceans, though a little trouble to prepare.

1 quart crayfish tails, cleaned,   Salt
parboiled and shucked   Pepper
1 egg   Cooking oil
1½ cups milk

Follow the usual procedure for breaking off the tails. Break the egg into a bowl, add milk, salt and pepper and mix thoroughly. Dip tails into the egg mixture, dust with flour and drop into deep fat pre-heated to 375 degrees. Cook until they are a golden brown, remove and drain on absorbent towel or paper. Serve on a large platter garnished with lemon slices and parsley. This dish may be accompanied by your favorite sauce to dip the tails into. If you haven't tried it, you are in for a pleasant surprise.

How to Clean a Turtle

Many people who happen while fishing to catch a large turtle either cut their lines out of fear, and return the turtle to the lake or stream, or throw it onto the bank to die and spoil. They do not realize that a turtle is excellent fare, from which a variety of tasty dishes can be prepared. Some people are also under the impression that to clean turtle is a major operation. But it is not really so complicated or difficult as all that.

There are more than a dozen species of fresh-water turtles, and many of them are caught for the commercial market. So are the giant sea turtles, which may weigh over a hundred pounds. A real treat if you are in one of the fishing villages of Baja California is to join a turtle barbecue, Mexican style. This special way of preparing the delicious meat of the turtle, once you taste it, is a feast you'll never forget.

Those who have eaten turtle often will tell you that there are several different kinds of turtle meat; a white part like that of a frog, a medium dark part similar to pork and another that looks like the dark meat of a chicken—all of them delicious.

Certain precautions should be taken in handling and cleaning a large live snapping turtle. With its powerful jaws and bill-like mouth it can very easily sever a finger or possibly even a hand. Begin by annoying the turtle so as to cause it to snap at a stick held in front of it. Once the beaklike mouth has taken hold, it will hang on. You can then pull the head and neck out of the shell and cut the head off with a hand axe. Hang up the turtle by the hind legs to bleed; since the heart continues to beat after decapitation, this will take at least an hour.

If possible, place the turtle whole in a tub of boiling water and continue boiling for fifteen or twenty minutes. This makes cleaning and skinning much easier. Remove the turtle from the water. When it is cool enough to handle, place it on its back, and with a short, stiff-bladed knife probe for a soft spot between the two shells. Insert the knife and cut around the edges through the skin where the two shells join. Then cut around and through the soft cartilaginous bridges of the back and underside, so as to separate the carcass into four quarters. These may be lifted out by inserting the knife underneath and lifting it up.

We suggest using a pair of fish-skinning pliers to skin out the legs, neck and tail, since they allow you to get a better grip on the tough, slippery skin. Be sure to save the large portion of meat at the base of the tail. Remove all the fat, and wash the meat thoroughly in a mild solution of salt water. Then disjoint and place in the refrigerator or freezer for future use.

Cut through outer skin and remove the belly plate.

Remove front legs and the neck from shell and body.

Remove rear legs from shell; use knife as wedge.

Front and hind legs skinned with fish-skinning pliers.

FRIED TURTLE

If you are fishing and happen to catch a good-sized soft-shelled turtle, this is the way to prepare it. Until you've learned how, the cleaning is admittedly rather difficult; but you will learn the trick with experience.

1 medium-sized turtle (will serve two persons)	½ teaspoon pepper
	2 bay leaves
1 teaspoon salt	Flour

Clean and disjoint the turtle into medium-sized pieces. Place in a stewing kettle with salt, bay leaves and pepper. Add enough water to cover the meat and let it boil for fifteen minutes. Let the turtle cool in the broth. Drain well, dust with salt, pepper and flour, and fry in a heavy skillet as you would chicken, until it is tender and golden brown. If desired, make a cream gravy from the residue in the skillet.

Serve with fluffy steamed rice, buttered asparagus tips and hot biscuits. As a salad we suggest pear halves with grated cheese; for dessert lemon pie.

TURTLE SOUP

A large bowl of delicious turtle soup is a most satisfying meal. You can feed more people on a small turtle in this way than any other.

To Prepare the Meat

One 2- or 3-pound turtle, cleaned	¼ teaspoon coarsely ground pepper
½ pound lean pork	2 bay leaves
½ teaspoon salt	½ teaspoon cumin

Place meat and seasonings in a large kettle, cover with water and simmer until the turtle meat is tender and can be removed from the bones. Remove all the meat and chop fine or cut into small cubes. Strain the liquid and save for stock.

To Make the Soup

3 cups turtle and pork meat chopped fine	2 medium-sized potatoes, finely diced
1 No. 303 can stewed tomatoes	4 carrots, cut into thin slices
	1 tablespoon pimento

Mix all the ingredients in a large stew pot, cover with turtle stock and simmer until the vegetables are done. Salt and pepper to taste. You will now have one of the very finest soups available.

This will make six large servings.

WHITEFISH COCKTAIL

The whitefish is very abundant in the Western states, especially Montana and Wyoming. It isn't as colorful as the Rainbow or Loch Leven trout, but caught on a fly rod in swift water it puts up an excellent fight.

Because of its high oil content, many people use it almost exclusively for smoking. We have also found it unsurpassed both for cocktails and for fish chowder.

1½ pounds whitefish (more if desired)	¼ teaspoon thyme
	Salt
2 bay leaves, crushed	Pepper
½ teaspoon rosemary	

Cut the whitefish approximately into thirds, place in a stew pot and cover completely with water. Add seasonings and bring to a boil. Cook ten minutes, remove from the fire and let the fish cool in the broth. Then, using your fingers, remove all the meat from the bones. In cocktail glasses place about two tablespoons of flaked meat per serving. Chill in the refrigerator. Just before serving, add cocktail sauce (see recipe on page 143).

If you have cooked more fish than necessary, place the remainder in a plastic bag and freeze for future use.

WHITEFISH CASSEROLE

1 cup cooked whitefish (see page 133 for directions on how to cook)

¼ medium-sized green pepper, sliced

1 rounded teaspoon sliced pimento

2 tablespoon butter or margarine

1 cup small elbow macaroni, cooked according to directions on the package

Sliced Cheddar cheese

Cornflake crumbs

Salt

Pepper

Lightly mix the cooked macaroni and fish. Add salt, pepper, pimento and green pepper, being careful not to break up the fish chunks. Put into a well buttered casserole, place sliced cheese on top, sprinkle on a layer of cornflake crumbs and dot with butter or margarine. Bake in a preheated oven at 300 degrees for approximately thirty minutes, or until the cheese melts and the contents are heated through.

Serve with lemon wedges, sweet pickle, carrot strips, celery and Italian garlic breadsticks.

This recipe provides an excellent lunch for four.

FRIED GRUNION

I suppose the grunion is the only edible fish that is caught with the bare hands—and on land! It is a small, silvery fish, rarely exceeding eight inches in length, and more often measuring six inches or less. Grunion are caught on ocean beaches a day or two after the full moon, at the time the tides are highest, when they come in on the waves to deposit their eggs in the sand. It is at this time that you can pick them up with your bare hands.

Grunion is an excellent food fish. Fried crisp, it is eaten bones and all. To prepare for cooking, scale and remove the heads. Sprinkle with salt and pepper, roll in corn meal and fry in a medium hot skillet until brown and crisp, being careful not to burn or overcook.

Serve with creamed corn, a green vegetable and a tossed green salad.

A hearty eater can eat six to eight of these small fish.

Part IV

APPETIZERS, SIDE DISHES
AND SAUCES

GRAPEFRUIT APPETIZER

Here is an appetizer that is sure to call forth favorable comment, and one that will get a game dinner off to a flying start.

Grapefruit cut crosswise, one
  half to a serving
For each half:
1 teaspoon Maraschino cherry
  juice
1 Maraschino cherry

1 rounded teaspoon dark
  brown sugar
1 teaspoon sherry cooking wine
½ teaspoon butter or
  margarine

Cut around the edge of each grapefruit half, being careful not to cut through the outer rind. Then cut around each section in order to loosen it, removing all the seeds.

Add the cherry juice, sugar, and sherry to each half, place a cherry in the center of each, and set in the refrigerator for one to two hours.

Before serving, dot with butter or margarine and bake in a preheated oven at about 250 degrees for about fifteen minutes. Serve piping hot.

BAKED ORANGES

As a special garnish for a game dinner, when you wish to make an impression on your family and guests we suggest this recipe.

4 thin-skinned seedless oranges   2 cups sugar

Wash the oranges, place in a kettle, cover with boiling water and cook until tender when tested with a fork. Remove from the water, cut in halves and arrange in a baking dish. Add the sugar to one cup of the water in which the oranges were boiled, and cook five minutes. Pour this syrup over the orange halves and dot with butter. Bake in a hot oven for about thirty minutes, or until the oranges are transparent.

GREEN BEANS SIMPLIFIED

We find this a delicious way to prepare beans. They can be cooking in the oven along with a roast. When the roast is done, the rest of the main course is also ready to go on the table.

1 No. 303 can green beans, drained (save the liquid)	1 strip bacon, cut into small pieces
2 green onions, chopped	Salt
¼ small green pepper, sliced or chopped	Pepper

Lay a sheet of aluminum foil approximately twenty-four inches long on a pie tin or shallow baking dish. Put the beans in the center; top with chopped onion, green pepper, bacon and salt and pepper to taste. Pour approximately one-fourth cup of bean liquid over the contents. Fold the aluminum foil, sealing all edges. Place in the oven with a roast or any other meat dish for approximately an hour.

This recipe will serve two persons.

FRIED CABBAGE

This recipe was given to us by a friend in Merced, California, and it is so good that we feel duty bound to pass it along. It is an especially fine complement to any broiled or pan-fried game.

½ medium-sized head cabbage, chopped	1 ounce pimento, sliced or chopped
3 slices bacon, chopped	3 or 4 tablespoons water
½ medium onion, chopped	Salt
	Pepper

Fry the chopped bacon in a skillet with the chopped onion. Add cabbage, pimento, salt, pepper and water. Cover and cook approximately ten to twelve minutes, or until the cabbage is tender. Do not overcook.

This recipe serves two.

VIRGINIA SPOON CORNBREAD

This recipe was given us by a friend who said the recipe had been in her family for so long that no one knew the origin of it. We find that it goes well with almost any meal.

4 eggs	1 teaspoon salt
2 cups milk	1 tablespoon sugar
1 cup corn meal	2 tablespoons melted butter or
2 tablespoons baking powder	vegetable shortening

Scald the milk in a double boiler. Add corn meal and salt, and continue to scald until the mixture thickens; then let it cool. Lightly beat the eggs and add them with the sugar to the corn meal mixture. Stir in the baking powder and melted shortening and pour into an ungreased casserole or deep baking dish. Bake in a moderate oven at 350 degrees until slightly brown, or for approximately one hour. Serve with a large tablespoon.

This recipe will serve four.

OLD-FASHIONED BUTTERMILK HOT CAKES

We use this recipe exclusively for hot cakes. It is simple and easy, and goes well with any game breakfast.

1½ cups flour	1 teaspoon baking powder
2 cups buttermilk	½ teaspoon baking soda
1 egg	2 tablespoons shortening
4 teaspoons sugar	¼ teaspoon salt

Put all the ingredients except the flour into a mixing bowl and blend with an eggbeater, making sure to dissolve the sugar and salt. Into another mixing bowl put the flour and slowly add the mixture to it, stirring constantly. If you prefer thin cakes, use all the liquid; if you want them thicker, use less milk.

This recipe will make about fifteen light, tender hot cakes, five or six inches in diameter. They should be cooked on a griddle or a heavy skillet, lightly greased.

ROGERS' DUMPLINGS

This dish is named for a very good friend, Mrs. Otis Rogers, who gave us the recipe. When we ate her chicken and dumplings, I was reminded of the ones an aunt of mine used to make when I was a boy in Arkansas. The recipe was no doubt brought direct from Oklahoma.

2 cups flour	½ teaspoon salt
1 cup shortening	⅛ pound butter or margarine
⅔ cup water	

Mix flour, shortening and salt, then add water and mix thoroughly. Place on a floured board and knead until the mixture is about as stiff as biscuit dough. Roll out to a thickness of about a quarter of an inch and cut into strips approximately half an inch wide and three inches long. Have plenty of meat broth ready. Bring it to a full rolling boil, add butter or margarine and drop dumplings into the pot one at a time. Do not stir, but use a fork to keep them from sticking. Cook for ten or twelve minutes.

HUSHPUPPIES

For us, no cookbook would be complete without an authentic recipe for Southern-style hushpuppies. This recipe came from a friend in Tennessee, but originated in Arkansas.

2 cups enriched corn meal	1 teaspoon pepper (if you wish,
¾ cup enriched flour	mix half and half with
4 teaspoons baking powder	cayenne pepper)
1 large onion chopped fine	2 large eggs
	Milk

Beat the eggs and mix all the ingredients thoroughly, slowly adding milk until the dough is thin enough to drop from a spoon in small amounts.

Fry the mixture in deep hot fat that has been used for fish or shrimp. Hushpuppies make any fish fry a huge success.

A MAN'S SALAD DRESSING

Any number of men, regardless of their culinary skill, have what they think is the world's best recipe for salad dressing. I am no exception. Here it is—a dressing I like very much, and one that is good on any tossed salad.

½ cup salad oil
¼ cup vinegar
½ teaspoon celery salt
½ teaspoon onion salt
¼ teaspoon rosemary leaves
1 teaspoon oregano
½ teaspoon garlic powder

Mix well and serve with greens, tomato and onion slices, or a salad of grapefruit and avocado.

ROQUEFORT DRESSING

Even though you can find some very good Roquefort dressings on the market, we think a good home-made dressing is nice for a change. This is a recipe we like very much.

¼ pound Roquefort or other blue cheese, crumbled
3 tablespoons milk or buttermilk
1 cup mayonnaise
¼ teaspoon paprika
6 tablespoons Wesson oil
Vinegar, salt and pepper to taste

Mix all the ingredients and whip until well blended.

COCKTAIL SAUCE

This is an excellent sauce for any fish or shrimp. We especially recommend it for a whitefish or trout cocktail.

1 cup tomato catsup	2 tablespoons chopped sweet
2 tablespoons lemon juice	pickle
1 teaspoon whole celery seed	½ teaspoon A-1 Sauce
¼ teaspoon prepared horse-	
radish	

Mix all ingredients thoroughly. Spoon approximately a tablespoonful over each cocktail just before serving.

HOT RELISH OR SAUCE FOR FISH

We call this a hot relish, though we eat so much highly seasoned food that it doesn't seem really hot to us. It is practically a must whenever we have a large fish fry. Besides going very well with the fish and pinto beans, it is also excellent with any venison roast.

1 one-pound, twelve-ounce can solid pack tomatoes, chopped	½ teaspoon oregano
1 medium-sized onion, chopped fine	½ teaspoon cumin
	Salt
1 seven-ounce can green chilies, chopped	Pepper

Mix all the above ingredients together and add salt and pepper to taste. Let stand thirty minutes or longer before serving. This sauce will keep several days in the refrigerator.

OPEN-PIT BARBECUE SAUCE

This barbecue sauce is one we often use for cooking the thinner cuts, especially the ribs, over open coals. It is easy and inexpensive, and gives a flavor you can get with no other sauce.

½ cup wesson oil, or olive oil if you prefer	1 teaspoon coarsely ground pepper
⅓ cup vinegar	1 tablespoon liquid smoke
1 teaspoon salt	3 tablespoons Worcestershire sauce

Combine all the ingredients and mix well with an eggbeater to blend and dissolve the salt. A little wine may be added if you like, though it is not necessary.

As you cook meat over open coals, baste frequently with this mixture.

SAUCE FOR A PIT BARBECUE

This tasty sauce is highly recommended for a pit barbecue, where for best results you should plan on using not less than twenty pounds of meat.

1 cup vinegar	1 teaspoon oregano
1 cup sherry wine	½ cup Worcestershire sauce
2 cups cooking oil	2 tablespoons salt
½ teaspoon cumin	½ teaspoon Tabasco sauce
1 teaspoon crushed rosemary leaves	1 cup finely chopped onions
1 teaspoon thyme	1 large can tomatoes
½ teaspoon black pepper	3 small cans green chilies
	1 can tomato paste

Mix all these ingredients well and heat until they are just about ready to boil. Remove from the flame and set aside to cool.

Part V

FROM FIELD TO FREEZER

What to Do After the Kill

It is to your advantage, when hunting deer or other game animals, to strive for a clean kill. You will ruin less meat, and the animal will undergo a painless death. If your gun is zeroed in and you are calm, try for a head or neck shot if conditions permit; otherwise a well-placed heart shot will drop an animal in its tracks. Such a shot will demolish its lung cavity and possibly penetrate the heart, causing the animal to bleed internally and obviating the necessity for cutting its throat.

When you have shot a deer, do not run up to it, knife in hand, ready to cut its throat. Approach the animal with caution, gun in hand, ready to fire in case it tries to charge you. If the animal's eyes are closed, look out—it is not dead. All large wild animals die with their eyes open, and even this is not a conclusive sign. Remember, the animal is fighting for survival, so be careful.

After you're sure the animal is dead, you may approach it. If it has been shot in the neck or head, it may be necessary to cut the throat for better bleeding. If so, place the head downhill so the blood will flow freely.

When the animal is fully bled, the first thing to do is to remove the genital organs. Place the animal on its back, and with a sharp knife cut under the penis, back to the rectum, removing the testicles as you work toward the back. To cut the genital organs loose it is not necessary to cut deeply into the meat, but you'll find they are connected to the pelvic bone by a tough ligament. In cutting this ligament, take care not to puncture the urethra and allow the contents of the bladder to flow over the meat.

Cut around the rectum, freeing the colon from the animal, pull out several inches and tie into a knot. This prevents the contents of the colon from falling on the meat.

Near the rear and center of the hind legs, make an incision large enough so you can insert the first and second fingers of the left hand. These act as a guide and also prevent the knife point from puncturing the intestines. Now, holding the knife in the right hand, and protecting the point with the fingers of the left hand, slowly cut the full length of the abdomen.

The next step is to cut the brisket. Use a fairly stiff knife or a small saw. Before cutting, slit the skin from the throat to the lower end of the brisket. Pull the skin back to avoid getting hair on the exposed meat. When the slit is completed, grasp the windpipe, pull it out as far as you can, and cut it loose. Now, with the knife or saw, cut through the full length of the brisket, turn the animal on its side, and pull out the internal organs. As you reach the diaphragm, which is a thick layer of tissue separating the chest and abdominal cavities, cut it loose and the entire stomach will come out easily. Reach into the chest cavity and pull out the lungs and heart and any remaining part of the windpipe.

When all the internal organs have been removed, turn the animal on its side, pick up one end, and spill out the accumulated blood. Wipe the cavity as clean and dry as possible with clean rags or paper towels. Place the heart and liver in a plastic bag.

If the deer or elk must be packed out of the area and will remain in the woods for several hours, hang it from a tree or place it over a fallen log or brush pile so it can cool. Be sure to pry apart the chest cavity and legs.

We did not cut the aitchbone—the bone of the rump—and hence some of the best meat will not be dried out. If you carefully cut around the rectum and pull the colon out, it is not necessary to cut the aitchbone.

There is some argument as to the advisability of removing the musk gland which is found on the hind hock of either sex. Those who do not recommend it contend that since the animal is dead and circulation has stopped, the gland's secretion cannot contaminate the meat. One precaution must be taken: Avoid getting this secretion on the hands or on the knife blade and touching the meat. Also, in skinning the animal, do not let the long, porous hairs of the musk gland, which are full of the secretion, come into contact with the meat.

Though you have taken good care of the meat in the field, additional cleaning will be necessary at home or camp. Hang the animal from a pole and with a generous amount of water, wash the inside thoroughly. Wipe as dry as possible and cover with a game bag of porous material such as cheese-cloth, to permit the free flow of air around the animal and to protect it from flies and other insects. Are you surprised that we said to wash the carcass with water? All government-inspected slaughter houses use hot water to clean domestic animals killed under far more favorable conditions than game. If you use water to wash away all foreign matter, you'll have a clean carcass ready to be processed.

When should the skin be removed? Opinions vary, but I never skin an animal until after it has aged ten days to two weeks, depending upon the weather. The skin protects the meat and keeps it moist until it has been aged. Then, when it is skinned and cut up for the freezer, it will be red instead of dark. The skin will not impart an undesirable flavor to the meat. However, on elk and moose, the hair is so thick around the neck, providing excellent insulation, that it is necessary to skin this portion of the animal to prevent the meat from souring.

In aging game with the hide on, cut the fore and hind legs off at the joints, cover the carcass with a highly porous bag and hang it in a cool, dry place protected from rain.

Skinning the Deer

There are numerous ways to skin a deer. Some people prefer to hang the animal by the hocks and skin down. Others hang the deer by the head, and some skin a small deer on a table or bench. I prefer to hang a deer by the hocks. If you follow the instructions, you will have meat for the freezer that has been properly prepared.

First, cut off the legs at the second joint. Cut the hind legs about an inch and a half below the joint. With a little practice this can be done quickly, but often a beginner may cut too high and sever the tendon, necessitating placing a wire on the bone to form a hock to hang by. Cut the forelegs only about an inch below the joint, bend back and cut through the skin and small tendons. Now, sever the head at the base of the skull, saving as much of the neck meat as possible. It's advisable to skin the legs several inches from the ends, then hang the carcass at a height convenient for your reach.

With a sharp knife, split the skin on the inside of the hams, down to the middle of deer, cutting in such a manner that the slit runs from leg to leg in one continuous cut. Start skinning with the knife, and when enough is peeled back, pull the hide with one hand and with the fist of other hand jab and punch between skin and animal. After the hams have been skinned, you can generally remove the hide to the shoulder blade with one continuous pull. By using this punch, jab, pull method you do not cut holes in the hide and you get less hair on the meat.

Now that the deer is approximately three-fourths skinned, slit the inside of the forelegs as you did the hind legs, and with knife and fingers, push and pull the hide free, being careful not to cut holes in it. When the forelegs are completely free, pull off the rest of the skin past the neck—and your deer is skinned.

No matter how careful you are in skinning the animal, some hair gets on the meat. It should be removed immediately, before the meat dries. To remove this hair, take a piece of freezer tape and pick up each hair. After one piece of tape is full of hair, discard it and get a new piece.

Now you may step back and admire an animal that has been properly cared for after the kill, properly aged and skinned, and is ready to be cut up for the freezer.

Butchering Your Kill

To butcher a deer properly, it is necessary to have the right tools. Listed below are all the tools needed to do a professional job.

> 1 butcher knife with at least a ten-inch blade
> 1 boning knife
> 1 steel for keeping knives sharp
> 1 meat saw
> 1 meat cleaver (optional)
> 1 roll freezer tape
> 1 roll freezer paper
> 1 roll Saran or similar wrap
> 1 marking pencil
> 1 strong table with cutting board

It will expedite matters considerably if one person cuts and one wraps and labels. With a little practice, you'll be surprised how quickly it can be done.

The basic cuts of a deer or other large animal are similar to a beef. (See chart showing basic cuts of meat). I do not follow this chart exactly in cutting a deer, but my method is fast and efficient and yields excellent roasts and steaks.

The first step is to split the animal down the middle of the backbone. To do this, hang the animal by the hocks at the height best suited to you and spread the legs as far apart as possible. Some prefer to work facing the inside of the animal, but I like to stand at the back and follow the featherbone with my saw.

Start sawing at the base of the tail, following the featherbone as closely as possible. Do not apply too much pressure to the saw, for doing so will cause it to veer left or right. Cut as straight as possible. As you approach the loin, the bone becomes thicker, and you are tempted to apply additional pressure to the saw. Don't! Continue to cut down through the neck bone.

Once the deer is cut in half, it must be quartered. This is done by cutting with the meat saw between the first and second ribs down to and through the backbone. Be careful not to let the front quarter drop to the floor. If cut correctly, the front quarter will weigh slightly more than the rear.

The Front Quarter

Let's start to cut up the front quarter first. Place it on the cutting table, inside down, and clean all hair and foreign matter from the meat. An old bath towel, slightly damp, is excellent for this. If the bullet penetrated the shoulder, be sure to trim away all bloodied meat. When the outside is clean, turn the front quarter and clean the inside, being sure to remove all dried, caked blood and all damaged meat from the bullet hole.

Grasp front leg at the end of the shank and lift up, and with the boning knife start cutting under the shoulder blade from the bottom and slightly to the rear and up, working in under the soft cartilage to the rear of the blade, and continue cutting upward and toward the backbone and forepart of the shoulder, with the cut ending and coming out just below the loin. There are no knuckle bones or other bones to saw to remove the shoulder, as it can be done entirely with the boning knife. When removed, turn the shoulder over with the inside up and remove the white, fatty-looking substance which is the gland. When it is all removed, cut the shank loose at the knuckle.

You now have a complete venison blade roast, and if the deer is of average size, it should be enough for four to six persons. If the deer is extra-large and your family is small, you can cut the blade in half, making two roasts, or cut a portion of it into chuck steaks, hamburger and stew meat.

This leaves the backbone with the neck and ribs still intact, so the next step is to cut the ribs off. Do this by cutting through the ribs crosswise about one inch below the loin, which is on the back next to the feather bone. This rib cage will make two meals for our family of two. I am amazed at the number of hunters who discard this portion of the deer. Some tasty dishes can be prepared from it, especially over a bed of charcoal. We usually cut this rib cage in half, crosswise, to make it easier to wrap and to fit in a baking pan, but it may be cut into about four-inch lengths.

This leaves only the backbone, which has the loin and the neck. The next move is to cut the neck off at the point where the top of the shoulder was. With the saw, cut through the vertebra of the neck, making slices about an inch thick, but do not cut through the meat. Leave the neck intact. If cut in this way, when cooked, each person may slice off a piece of neck meat.

The only part left of the front quarter is the backbone, on which is the loin, the finest part of the animal for steaks. You can cut it into chops, or you can remove the loin from the back and feather bone. If you cut it into chops, cut them thick enough to be tasty. However, many people remove the loin. It's easy to do, and you will have delicious breakfast steaks.

With the boning knife, cut down the edge and side of the feather bone to the point where the ribs join the backbone. Do this the full length of the loin, staying as close to the bone as possible to avoid leaving much meat. When you have cut to the end, start at the front, and placing the knife on the rib, cut up to the base of the backbone and feather bone. After cutting back a few inches, you can hold the meat up with one hand, cutting next to the bone and cutting off all the meat. If you prefer, you may leave the strip of loin in one piece, freeze it, and when you want steaks, cut them off then. Cut the steaks fairly thick. We label this cut "Venison Loin Breakfast Steaks." They are excellent with eggs, and for a real treat, serve them with cream gravy and hot biscuits.

What should you do with the shank? Most hunters cut it up for stew meat. It makes better stew than hamburger meat. We leave the meat on the bone, wrap it well and put it in the freezer, and later have Venison Shank à la Montana.

The Hind Quarter

From the hind quarter of the deer, you will get most of your steaks and some fine roasts. The hind quarter is no more difficult to cut up than the front quarter.

First, place the quarter on a table with the inside up. Again, as with the front quarter, remove all foreign material, such as dried blood, hair, etc. Use a moistened bath towel and rub briskly, then use a knife to scrape off the remains. If this doesn't clean the meat, cut thin slices to remove the hair and blood. When the meat is clean, trim off all excess fat. It will be quite thick on the rump; in fact, on some large Montana bucks, the fat is often two and a half inches thick, and some are completely covered with a thin layer of fat. Though such an amount of fat is indicative that the animal is healthy and that the meat will be juicy and tender, do not cook the deer with the fat on it. Trim it off and replace with beef suet when a fat is desired.

Now that the meat is clean, start by trimming off the flank meat. There is a lot of good lean meat here, with some fat which should be removed. Some add beef suet to the flank and make a rolled roast, but I prefer to use it in hamburger meat.

By now we have worked down to some of the best meat on the hind quarter—the sirloin tip. This is the portion just above the knee. Though it is muscular, it is not used much and is very tender. Some prefer to make a roast from the tip, but I like to cut it into small steaks for breakfast. If used for a roast, be sure to add some beef suet to it to avoid dryness. If you're undecided as to whether you want it cut into steaks, or left as a roast, freeze it as a roast and later let the occasion determine how you want to cook it.

After finishing with the sirloin tip, the next step is to cut the loin from the buttock. To do this, place the saw at the bottom of the rump, pointing toward the last joint in the tail. Saw through all the bone structure and finish the cut with your knife. The buttock, or ham as it is often called, is all muscle. These muscles are used in walking, climbing and running, so it might be slightly tough, but slow cooking with moisture will alleviate the condition, especially if the pot is covered.

Now that the loin has been removed from the buttock, you are confronted with the same problem as with the front quarter: Shall you remove the loin or cut it into T-bones or porterhouse steaks? Make the decision and proceed accordingly, removing the loin the same way as you did on the front quarter.

The tenderest part of the entire animal is the tenderloin. I often refer to it as the "hanging tenderloin" because it hangs from the backbone, one on each side. It is located to the extreme rear, protected from the backbone on one side and a lot of kidney fat on the other. It's only about two inches in diameter and approximately twelve inches long. To remove it, proceed much as you did to remove the top loin. It may be sliced crosswise and made into delicious small steaks, or split lengthwise and folded out, leaving the two pieces joined together. They are excellent when cooked over charcoal or broiled and basted with butter.

This leaves the round, and it's best to bone it. With a boning knife, start at the shank knuckle and cut all the way through the meat to the top of the bone where it joins at the rump knuckle. Use your fingers to spread the meat and feel for the bone and you should have no difficulty. Cut under the bone, which is discarded when completely cut from the meat.

When the bone has been removed, locate a seam in the ham with your fingers and pull the meat apart. Use a knife to cut the few pieces of meat holding it together. As you spread these two pieces apart, you'll notice a fatty, white substance. This is the "kernel," often referred to in the recipes for small game animals. Be sure to remove this "kernel" before freezing and cooking.

After separating the ham at the seam, you have two nice venison roasts which may be cut into steaks. From the eye of the round you can cut some nice little steaks comparable to those you cut from the sirloin tip.

As you work down to the lower part of the round, the meat is more muscular and tough. This should not be cut into steaks or roasts, but cut into stew or hamburger meat. Some hunters, when processing a deer—whether at home or in a processing plant—grind the burger at this time. I suggest that, when trimming the meat and saving the trimming, you take special precautions to see that it is kept clean and only *good* meat is included. Discard blood-shot meat or meat with tissue broken from the impact of the bullet. Don't grind it at this time, but place it in plastic bags in one- or two-pound packages, depending upon the size of your family. Later, if you wish to make stew, take out the necessary amount and use it as is. If you wish to make meat loaf, stuffed peppers or hamburgers, grind it as you use it, adding about twenty per cent beef suet to each pound of venison.

Preparing Meat for the Freezer

Even if you have done an excellent job of field dressing and butchering a game animal, much of your work can be ruined unless you take certain simple precautions in preparing it for the freezer.

Freezer burn is the biggest problem. We first wrap our meat with Saran wrap or similar pliofilm. Because of its excellent meat-clinging qualities, this wrap excludes all the air from around the meat. When this is done, we wrap with freezer paper, using the drugstore wrap, for we have found this makes a much neater package and uses less paper. With a little practice one soon becomes proficient.

At least twenty-four hours before the meat is to be put in the freezer, turn the dial to maximum coldness. Do not put all the meat in at once so as not to overload the box, allowing small batches of meat to freeze as quickly as possible. Place the packages in the freezer in a crisscross fashion so air may circulate freely around them, hastening the freezing process. When you put packages of meat in the freezer for final storage, try to arrange them according to cuts—the roasts together, steaks together, etc. Also, place them with the labeled side up so you can find a particular cut without opening the packages.

Small plastic bags are ideal for packaging stew meat. These bags are especially suitable for wrapping liver, as it is so slippery. Put the meat in the bags, squeeze out all air, then wrap with paper, label and date.

Preparing moose round roast for freezer. Pliofilm wrap clings to meat, excludes air.

Roast is then wrapped in freezer paper using the neat drug-store wrap.

Finish wrapping job by applying masking tape to hold turned-over ends of package.

Label contents of package and place in freezer with the label side up.

Should I Take My Game
to a Processing Plant?

"Should I try to butcher and wrap my deer, or should I take it to a processing plant?" Many hunters have asked themselves that question. For some hunters the fun is over after they have done a halfway job of field dressing the animal. They let someone else take care of the meat from there on. For others, processing and wrapping their game is as much fun as the actual hunt. If they are so situated that they can work in a corner of the garage or some other sheltered place, they can cut and wrap each package according to the needs of their family. Not only that, they may wish to bone all the meat and save valuable space in the freezer.

Let's look at some facts and figures before going to a processing plant; then you can make your own decision.

First, the minimum cost will be about $.08 per pound for cutting and wrapping, plus $1.50 or more plus the hide for skinning. This price is based on the weight of the deer as you brought it in, perhaps with head, feet and skin still on animal.

We've heard many hunters complain they did not get all their meat back from the processing plant, accusing the butcher of keeping the choice cuts. This isn't necessarily so. Let's assume your deer weighed 150 pounds when it arrived at the processing plant.

Head with antlers	27 lbs.
Hide	18
Feet	6
Loss from blood shot and damage	5
	56 lbs.
Meat left to cut and wrap	94
	150 lbs.

There is your deer—head, feet and skin removed—leaving you a net amount of 94 pounds to be cut, wrapped, labeled and frozen. Now, let us do some more figuring on the cost of processing and see how you can save a few dollars.

150 pounds @ .08	$12.00
Cost of skinning	1.50
Total cost for processing	$13.50

Let's assume you are going to skin the animal yourself. Look at the saving you make by doing it.

156

Removing head	27 lbs.	@ $.08	$2.16
Removing skin	18 lbs.	@ $.08	1.44
Removing feet	6 lbs.	@ $.08	.48
Removing damaged meat	5 ·lbs.	@ $.08	.40
Fee saved by skinning			1.50
Total saved			$5.98
Original cost of processing			13.50
New cost if you skin deer			$7.52

You can see that you save $5.98 and retain the hide to be tanned for your own personal use.

If you have cleaned and skinned your deer yourself and intend to take it to the processing plant to be cut and wrapped, we wish to caution you. Before leaving the carcass at the plant, check the holding room and see how much game is waiting to be processed. Is it overloaded and the temperature higher than it should be? Does it have a peculiar odor, as if some of the game might be spoiled or sour? If such is the case, do not leave your game to be hung in this room, for in a few hours it will have absorbed some of the odor.

The processing plant is not entirely to blame for this condition. Many hunters bring in their game from the out-camps, much of it improperly field dressed. Some game has hung so long in warm weather it has already soured. Flies have deposited their eggs in some of the deer while it was in the out-camps. So much warm meat placed in a small holding room at once overloads the refrigeration plant, causing some of the other meat to sour.

Such processing plants are in the minority, however, for most of them take pride in their work. As soon as a responsible plant is loaded to capacity, it turns down additional game until such time as it can give it proper care.

If the processing plant cannot cut and wrap your deer immediately, take it home. Perhaps you can persuade your butcher to cut it up for you; then you can wrap and label it yourself.

Now you can judge the advantages and disadvantages of taking your game to a processing plant, and you may make your own decision. For the past ten years I've processed all our game, but I'm fortunate in having an electric meat saw and grinder, an assortment of good knives, other tools, and a well-protected place in which to work. I usually do a quarter or a half at a time, unless I'm rushed; and if I'm pressed for freezer space, I bone practically all my meat.

INDEX

INDEX